This book is to be returned on or before the last date below.

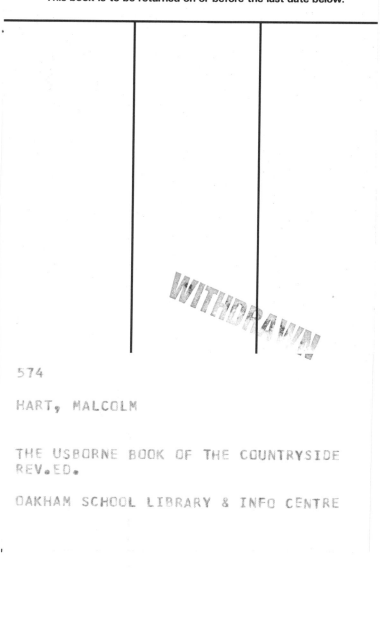

THE USBORNE
BOOK OF THE
COUNTRYSIDE

Contents

Malcomn Hart, Ingrid Selberg, Sue Tarsky and Margaret Stephens

Consultant editors: Peter Holden, Sally Heathcote
Jean Mellanby, E, H, M, Harris

Designed by Amanda Barlow, Robert Walster and Diane Thistlethwaite

Edited by Sue Jacquemier

Illustrated by Mike Atkinson, Graham Austin, Andrew
Beckett, Dave Ashby, John Barber, David Baxter,
Isabelle Bowring, Hilary Burn, Liz Butler, Patrick
Cox, Christine Darter, John Francis, Victoria Gordon,
Tim Hayward, Christine Howes, Ian Jackson,
Colin King, Deborah King, Ken Lilly , Malcolm Mcgregor,
Richard Millington, David Nash, Barbera Nicholson, Charles Raymond
(Virgil Pomfret Agency), Gwen Simpson, Joyce
Tuhill, Phil Weare, Roger Kent and Gillian Platt
(The Garden Studio)

The material in this book is also published as
three separate titles in the Usborne Nature Trail series:
Birdwatching, Trees and Leaves and Wildflowers.

First published in 1976 by Usborne Publishing Ltd, 83-85 Saffron Hill, London, EC1N 8RT, England. Revised
1993. Copyright © 1993. 1985, 1976 Usborne Publishing Ltd.

Bluetit

Nuthatch

If you are walking along a seashore, rambling in the countryside or sitting in a city garden, you can alway find birds. This section of the book will help you to identify them and give you lots of information about their habits.

When you go bird spotting take this book with you and turn to the pages which deal with the kind of place you are visiting, such as a wood or pond. Pages 28-31 will give you extra help by showing you the size of certain birds.

The birds on these pages are not drawn to scale

Chaffinch

BIRDWATCHING

Contents

Stonechat

Siskin

How to be a birdwatcher

The most important thing to have when you go birdwatching is a notebook. If you try and keep all the facts in your head, you will probably forget some of the important ones.

Make sure any notes you make are clear and readable. The picture on the right shows how to set your notebook out. Try to draw the birds you see. Even a bad drawing is better than no drawing at all.

Notes on shape, size, colour and flight pattern will be important later, if you need to identify a bird.

A birdwatcher has to take notes quickly. Use a spiralbound notebook, like the one here. It has a stiff back to help you write easily. File your notes away in date order when you get home or write them up into a neat book. When you are out, put your notebook in a plastic bag to keep it dry.

Look carefully for the shape and obvious marks first. The male Reed Bunting here has a sparrow-like body and beak, a dark head, white collar and white outer tail feathers. It also has a dark throat and dark flecks on its side.

Male Reed Bunting

Black head
White collar
Grey-white underneath

2nd August 1991
Weather - Sunny
Clare Park
M Reed Bunting

Dark Brown streaked back

Also
F carrying grass
(for * ?)

Flight Pattern

Make sure you have all the details of place, date, time of day and weather entered in your notebook.

Bird shorthand

M	=	MALE
F	=	FEMALE
JUV	=	JUVENILE (YOUNG BIRD NOT IN ADULT FEATHERS)
*	=	NEST
C10	=	ABOUT TEN (WHEN TALKING ABOUT NUMBERS OF BIRDS)

Use these signs instead of writing out the words. It will save you time. Always take two pens or pencils with you.

How to stalk birds

In the countryside there is plenty of opportunity to see many types of birds. When you go birdwatching camouflage your shape by standing in front of or behind a tree or bush. Keep the sun behind you, so you are in shadow. If there is no cover, crawl closer using your elbows and feet. Don't wear clothes that rustle when you move. Never move quickly in the open.

Green Woodpecker

Willow Warbler

Woodcock

What to wear

Travel as light as possible. Remember to wear dull colours.

Hat or hood.

Anorak or warm coat.

Wellingtons if wet. Trainers at all other times.

Notebook and pencils.

Buying binoculars

Choose the lightest pair you can find. The best size to get is 8 x 30 8 x 40.

Binocular strap

Belt

String tied to strap and belt.

Binoculars

Binoculars are not essential for birds in the garden or park. But if you want some, go shopping with a person who knows about binoculars. However light your binoculars are, they will start to feel heavy after a while. To take the weight off your neck, you can tie some string onto the strap as shown here.

Quick field sketches

1 Two circles for head and body.

2 Add beak, neck, tail and legs.

3 Add details of feathers.

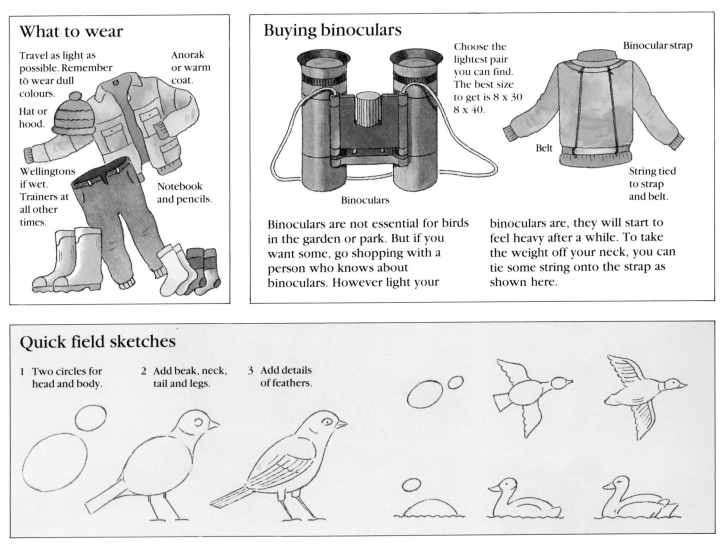

The best way to make notes on the birds you see is to draw quick sketches of them. Begin by drawing two circles - one for the body and one for the head.

Notice the size and position of the head and body before you start. Add the tail, beak, legs and then add details of feathers if you have time. Do not draw what you do not see. Practise by drawing the birds you can see from your window or sit on a bench in the park and draw the birds there.

Remember to use your ears as well as your eyes. Birdsong is very important when you go birdwatching. It is often the first clue to tell you that a bird is near. The Jay, pictured here, has a very raucous call . Other sounds can give you clues too. You will often hear a Green Woodpecker drilling a hole in a tree before you see it.

You will not get far loaded with heavy equipment and you will be unable to move easily and quietly. If birds can see your shape silhouetted against the sky, they will fly off.

Chaffinch

Nuthatch

Jay

Chaffinch

What to look for

These pages tell you what to look for when you want to identify a bird.

When you see a bird for the first time, there are several questions you should ask. What size is it? Has it any obvious marks, such as the Reed Bunting's black head and white outer tail feathers? How does it fly and feed? How does it behave? Where is it? What colour is it?

Sometimes differences in colour can be confusing. There are some examples of this on the page opposite.

Rounded wings with slight "fingers".

This is a female Sparrowhawk chasing a male Reed Bunting. The labels give examples of the kind of thing to note down when you see a bird.

Hooked beak

Long tail with dark bars.

Black head

White collar

White outer tail feathers.

Yellow legs

Flight patterns

Buzzard

Chaffinch

Mallard

When you see a bird, notice how it flies. Does it bounce in flight like the Chaffinch? Does it float and soar like the Buzzard, or fly fast and straight like a Mallard?

Shapes in flight

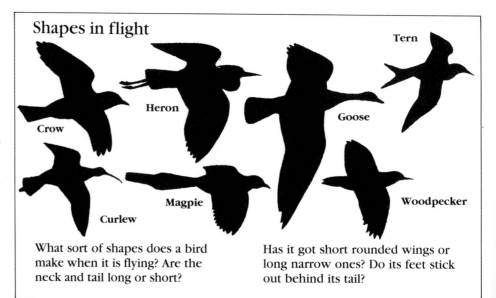

Tern

Heron

Goose

Crow

Magpie

Woodpecker

Curlew

What sort of shapes does a bird make when it is flying? Are the neck and tail long or short?

Has it got short rounded wings or long narrow ones? Do its feet stick out behind its tail?

Sex differences

Male

Female

Blackbirds

The males of some birds, such as the Blackbird, have different coloured feathers and beaks from the females.

Colour changes

Summer

Winter

Black-headed Gulls

Some birds, such as the Black-headed Gull, have a different plumage in winter from the plumage they have in summer.

Age differences

Adult   Juvenile (young)

Robins

In some birds, such as the Robin, the young look very different from their parents.

Looking at beaks

Carrion Crow

Greenfinch

Curlew

Grey Heron

Beaks can give you clues to what a bird eats. The Carrion Crow's beak is an all-purpose tool. The Greenfinch's beak is more suited to eating seeds.

The Curlew uses its long beak to probe for food in mud. The Grey Heron's beak is even longer and is used to catch fish, frogs and insects.

One way to identify a bird is from its song. Go out with someone who knows birdsong well, or borrow records of birdsong from your library

Watch what birds are doing

Grey Wagtail

Treecreeper

Turnstone

The Grey Wagtail often patrols in mud or short grass. It wags its tail up and down. Sometimes it makes a dash after an insect.

The Treecreeper creeps up the trunk of a tree, picking out insects from cracks in the bark with its thin, curved bill.

The Turnstone walks along the beach turning over seaweed and stones, looking for small creatures, such as shellfish, to eat.

Clues and tracks

Sometimes you may not be able to see all the birds that live in an area. Even if you don't see them, special clues can tell you they are present. Some of these clues are easy to spot, such as feathers and the remains of meals.

You may not be able to identify the feathers you find straight away. But later you may see a dead bird, or a bird in a book, that has feathers like the ones you have collected. Remember that most birds have feathers of many different sizes and colours.

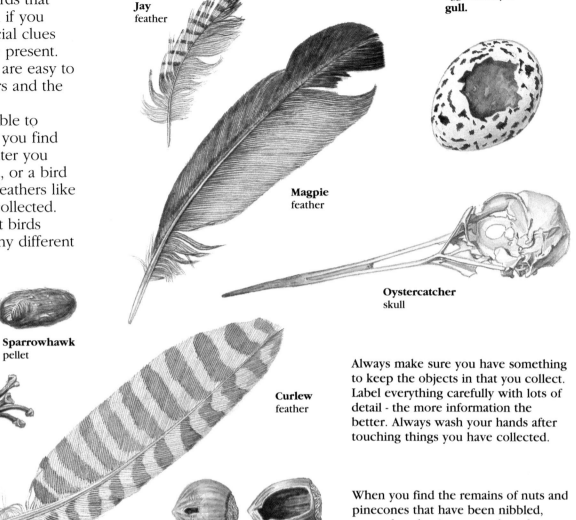

Jay
feather

Magpie
feather

Sandwich Tern
egg eaten by a **gull.**

Oystercatcher
skull

Jackdaw
pellet

Sparrowhawk
pellet

Pine cone
nibbled by
a **squirrel.**

Curlew
feather

Hazelnut pecked at
by a **Great Tit.**

Hazelnut pecked at
by a **Woodpecker.**

Always make sure you have something to keep the objects in that you collect. Label everything carefully with lots of detail - the more information the better. Always wash your hands after touching things you have collected.

When you find the remains of nuts and pinecones that have been nibbled, remember that it may not have been a bird. Squirrels and mice eat these as well. So, be careful when you identify the nibbler.

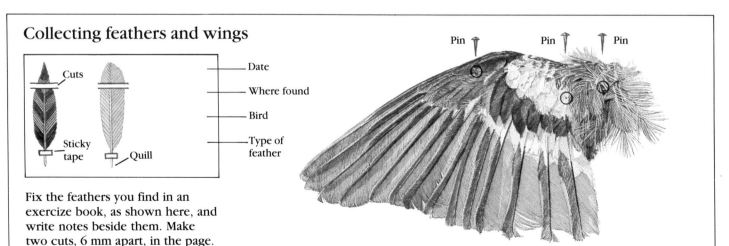

Collecting feathers and wings

Cuts

Sticky
tape

Quill

Date

Where found

Bird

Type of
feather

Pin

Pin

Pin

Fix the feathers you find in an exercize book, as shown here, and write notes beside them. Make two cuts, 6 mm apart, in the page. Thread the feather through and then stick the quill down with sticky tape.

Wings cut from dead birds can be dried and kept. Pin the wing out on a piece of stiff board. It should dry

in a few days and can then be placed in an envelope with a label and some mothballs.

Pinecones

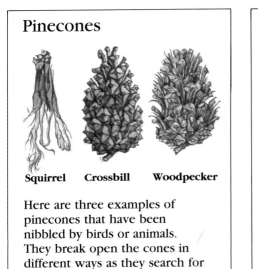

Squirrel   **Crossbill**   **Woodpecker**

Here are three examples of pinecones that have been nibbled by birds or animals. They break open the cones in different ways as they search for seeds to eat.

Nuts

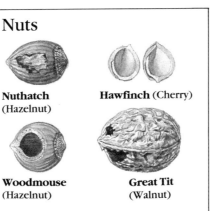

Nuthatch (Hazelnut)   **Hawfinch** (Cherry)

Woodmouse (Hazelnut)   **Great Tit** (Walnut)

Animals all have their own ways of opening nuts. Mice chew neat little holes, while some birds leave jagged holes and others split the nuts in half.

The Song Thrush's anvil

Snail shell

Broken shells

Anvil

Song Thrushes use a stone like an anvil to break open snail shells. Look for the anvil - it will be surrounded by the remains of the bird's meal.

Owl pellets

Contents of one owl pellet.

Owls swallow small animals and birds whole, and then cough up the fur, feathers and bones as a pellet. You can find these beneath trees or posts where the owl rests. Pull a pellet apart and sort out the bones. The easiest bones to identify are the skulls of animals the owl has eaten.

Other pellets

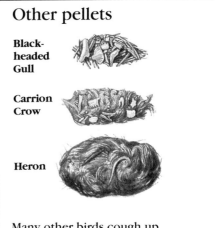

Black-headed Gull

Carrion Crow

Heron

Many other birds cough up pellets. But it is harder to identify what is inside them, as most birds do not eat large animals.

Footprint casts

Water

Plaster of Paris

Bird footprint

Ring of cardboard.

Pour in plaster mixed with water.

Paint when plaster cast is set.

Put the cardboard around the footprint. Mix the plaster in the cup and pour it into the ring. Let it harden for 15 minutes. Take the cast and its cardboard home.

To make plaster casts you will need water, plaster of Paris, a plastic cup or glass and a strip of cardboard bent into a ring, and fastened with a paperclip.

Wash off any dirt. Leave the cast for a few more days to dry thoroughly and then carefully remove it from the cardboard. Paint the footprint and then varnish it.

Making a bird garden

On these pages you can see many of the birds that visit gardens or window sills for food. Different kinds of food attract different birds. Put out bones, suet, cheese, oats, peanuts, currants and bits of bacon rind. Scatter some food in the open though for birds that prefer to eat on the ground. A good way of attracting birds is by building a bird bath and a bird table for your garden.

Feeding chart

Make a chart of the kinds of food you see different birds eating. Which birds like nuts best? Tick the boxes each time you see a bird eat something.

Soon you will know which foods are popular and can make sure they are always in the garden.

Key to birds

1 **Greenfinch**
2 **House Sparrow**
3 **Blue Tit**
4 **Robin**
5 **Coal Tit**
6 **Starling**
7 **Chaffinch**
8 **Blackbird**
9 **Mistle Thrush**
10 **Goldfinch**
11 **Song Thrush**
12 **Dunnock**
13 **Bullfinch**

Putting out food

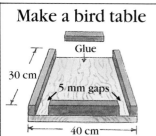

Thin thread

Darning needle

Matchstick

Yogurt pot

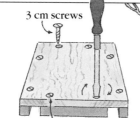

Melt the fat in a warm oven.

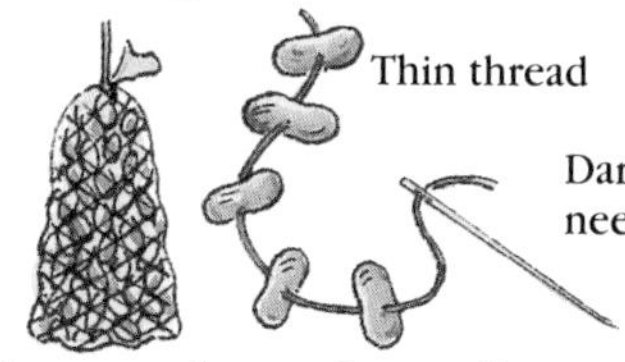

Supermarkets often sell vegetables in nets. Fill one of these with unsalted peanuts, or thread peanuts in their shells on thread or thin string, and hang them up in the garden.

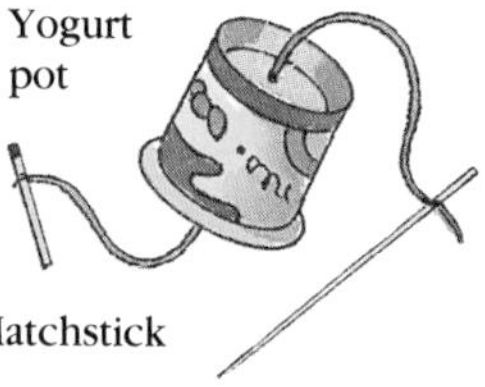

Make a feeding bell with a yogurt pot. Fill the pot with breadcrumbs, currants, cooked potato and oatmeal. Ask an adult to help you melt some fat.

Let it cool and then pour it on the mixture. Wait until it hardens and then pull some thread through it as shown in the picture. Hang it upside down with the thread.

Make a bird table

Glue

30 cm

5 mm gaps

40 cm

3 cm screws

Put screws in under batten strips.

Gaps let rain water drain off.

You will need a piece of outdoor quality plywood about 40 cm x 30 cm and four strips of batten about 30 cm long. Glue the battens to the plywood as shown above.

When the glue has dried, turn the table over and put in two screws on every side, as shown above. Protect your table with a wood preservative and screw it to a wooden box.

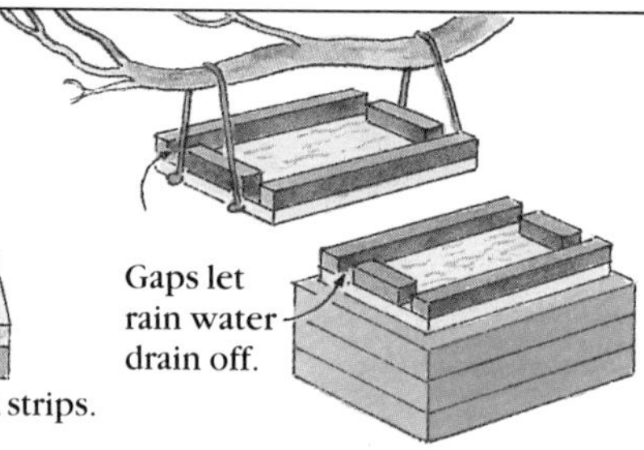

To make a hanging table, put four screw-eyes into the sides and use string to hang it from a branch, as shown above. Clean the table regularly with disinfectant.

Make a bird bath

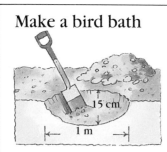

15 cm

1 m

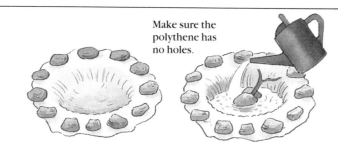

Make sure the polythene has no holes.

Choose a place not too close to the feeding area you have set up. Dig a hole with sloping sides, about 15 cm deep and 1 m wide. Dig from the middle out.

Line the hole with strong polythene (a dustbin liner will do). Weight the polythene down with stones and sprinkle gravel or sand over the lining.

Put a few stones and a short branch in the middle to make a perch. Fill the bath with water. Keep it full and make sure it is free from ice in winter.

7

8 Female

10

10

7 Male

Plants that birds like to eat

Shepherd's Purse

Ivy

Rowan   Groundsel

Hawthorn

Thistle

Wild grasses   Elder   Cotoneaster

All these plants are good bird food. If you have a garden, try to let a little patch grow wild. Weeds, such as Groundsel, have seeds that birds like to eat. Trees and bushes, such as Rowan, have lots of good berries in the autumn. Some birds like over-ripe apples and sultanas. Dig over a patch of earth, so you make it easier for some birds to find worms and insects.

9

9

9

2 Male

1

4   3

3   3

5

2 Female

2 Male

1   3   3

12

6

1

7 Female

8 Male   4

7 Male

13 Male

2 Female

13 Female

11   12   6

Making a nesting box

Encourage birds to visit your garden in spring by building a nesting box. If the entrance hole is small then a Blue Tit will probably nest there. If the hole is larger then you may find a House Sparrow using it.

Other birds, such as Great Tits, Starlings, Tree Sparrows and Wrens, sometimes use nesting boxes. Try not to go close up to the box if birds are nesting there, as you will frighten them away. You can always watch them from indoors.

To make your nesting box you will need some plywood that is 12 mm thick with an overall length of 900 mm and width of 254 mm.

Side removed to show how box is made.

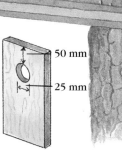

How to cut the wood

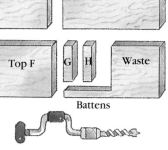

| A Back | B Front | C Base | Waste |

| 241 ↑ D Side 102 ← 254 → | 254 ↑ E Side 102 ← 241 ↓ | Top F | G | H | Waste |

J Main support

Battens

First cut the pieces in these sizes

A 254 mm x 127 mm
B 241 mm x 127 mm
C 127 mm x 127 mm
D See diagram
E See diagram
F 152 mm x 127 mm
G 102 mm x 25 mm
H 102 mm x 25 mm
J 510 mm x 25 mm

Drill the entrance hole with a hand drill about 50 mm from the top of the front section. The hole should be 25 mm wide.

50 mm

25 mm

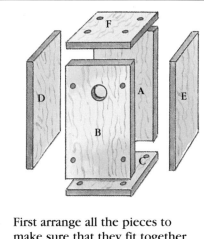

First arrange all the pieces to make sure that they fit together properly. Then drill holes for all the screws.

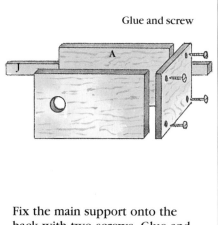

Glue and screw

Fix the main support onto the back with two screws. Glue and screw the bottom onto the back and then the front.

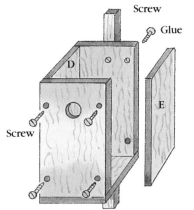

Screw

Glue

Screw

Glue and then fit the side pieces into place. Screw them on if they fit properly. If they don't, check the measurements carefully.

Where to put the box

Your completed nesting box should be fixed to a tree trunk or to a wall that is covered with a climbing plant, such as ivy. If there is no climbing plant, a bare wall or tree trunk will do. The entrance hole should not face south or west as the heat from direct sunlight might kill the young birds. Fix it about 2 m or more above the ground, well away from cats. Every winter, take it down and empty out the old nest. Disinfect the box and give it a new coat of wood preservative before replacing it.

2 m

Box must face north or east.

Other types of box

Special nesting boxes can be bought for House Martins. You can fix them under the edge of the roof.

100 mm

Side removed to show how box is made.

An open-fronted box is good for other birds. Make it like the first box, but cut an opening as shown in the picture above.

Keeping a record

Try to make a note of what happens in your nesting box. If a bird nests in the box there will be many details to record throughout the spring and summer.

You may even see some birds visiting the box in winter. They use boxes to sleep in. The notes below tell you the sort of thing to record.

1 Date of first visit.
2 Number of birds visiting.
3 Date bird first enters box.
4 Date birds bring nest material.
5 Type of nest material.
6 Date birds first bring food.
7 Type of food.
8 Date young leave nest.

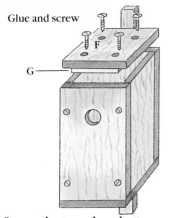

Glue and screw

F

G

Screw the two short battens on the underside of the box's lid. Make sure the removable lid fits tightly and securely.

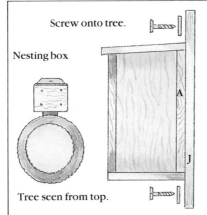

Screw onto tree.

Nesting box

A

J

Tree seen from top.

Paint the outside of the box with wood preservative and let it dry. Screw or nail it on to a tree (see above).

BLACKBIRD
First visit Feb 22nd
2 birds
First entered box
23rd Feb.
Nesting material
March 1st.

The nesting season

The nesting season is a time of great activity for all birds. First they must find a mate and then start looking for a place to build a nest and feed. The spot they choose becomes their territory. Next they lay their eggs and rear their young.

With all this going on it is not difficult to find out where some birds are building a nest or feeding their young. A bird carrying something in its beak, such as worms or grass, is the most common sign. On these pages you will find some more clues to help you.

A parent Song Thrush arrives at the nest. The young birds beg for food with wide open mouths. The parent puts food into their mouths and then flies off on another food-hunting expedition.

Food chart

Make a food chart to record which birds you see carrying food to their young, and record the type of food.

	WORMS	SNAILS	INSECTS
BLACKBIRD			
ROBIN			
SONG THRUSH			

Remember - it is against the law to disturb breeding birds or their nests and eggs. Always watch from a distance.

14

Spotting nesting birds

Rook

Nightingale

Droppings

Stonechat

In the spring, you will often see birds carrying nest material in their beaks. Rooks break off large twigs to make their nests.

Look out and listen for a bird singing in the same place every day during spring and summer, such as the Nightingale. It is probably breeding.

You may see adult birds carrying droppings away from the nest in their beaks. They do this to keep the nest clean for their young.

Nest materials

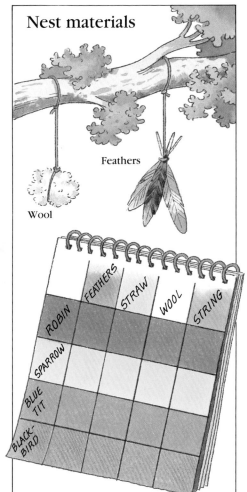

Feathers

Wool

	FEATHERS	STRAW	WOOL	STRING
ROBIN				
SPARROW				
BLUE TIT				
BLACK-BIRD				

Hang up bits of wool, feathers, straw and string from a tree. Make a note of what different materials birds collect to use for their nests.

Where birds nest

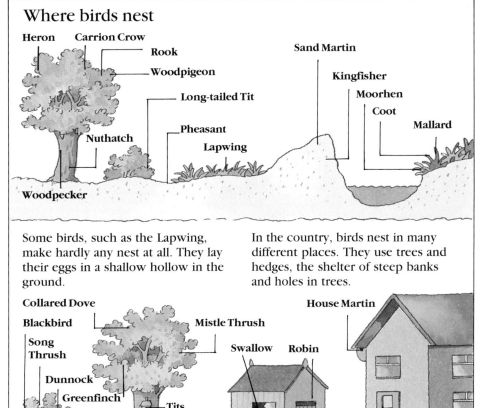

Heron   Carrion Crow
Rook
Woodpigeon
Long-tailed Tit
Sand Martin
Kingfisher
Moorhen
Coot
Mallard
Pheasant
Lapwing
Nuthatch
Woodpecker

Some birds, such as the Lapwing, make hardly any nest at all. They lay their eggs in a shallow hollow in the ground.

In the country, birds nest in many different places. They use trees and hedges, the shelter of steep banks and holes in trees.

Collared Dove
Blackbird
Song Thrush
Dunnock
Greenfinch
Wren
Mistle Thrush
Swallow   Robin
Tits
House Martin

Many birds nest in gardens, but only in sheltered places safe from cats and dogs. They use thick bushes, trees, ivy-covered walls and sheds,

as well as nesting boxes. Other birds, such as the House Martin, build under the roof, and Barn Owls can nest on a ledge in an old barn.

Ponds and inland waterways

Ducks are the birds you are most likely to see on a pond. They have quite long necks, webbed feet and wide, flat bills. They are all good swimmers. Most ducks feed on water plants in the pond.

Ducks can be divided into three kinds. There are diving ducks, such as the Tufted Duck, and dabblers, such as the Mallard. The most rare are the fish-eating ducks called sawbills.

In spring and summer, you will often see ducklings trailing behind their parents on the water's surface, or even hitching a piggy-back ride.

Swimming

Shoveler   **Coot**   **Moorhen**

Webbed feet are best for swimming. The web opens to push hard against the water. When the foot comes back. the web closes so that the foot does not drag through the water.

Coots and Moorhens spend more time on land. Coots' feet are partly webbed. Moorhens have hardly any webbing. Their heads jerk backwards and forwards when the birds swim.

New ducklings are taken to the water by their mother. The ducklings fall in and can swim straight away.

Male and female Mallards have a blue flash on each wing called a speculum.

Great Crested Grebes are fish eaters. The male and female both look after their chicks, carrying them on their backs.

Female Mallard

Male Mallard

Long, flat bills are useful to sift food.

How water birds feed

Swallow catching insects over the water.

Pintail up-ending.

Kingfisher diving for fish.

Tufted Duck diving.

Wigeon grazing on land.

Moorhen feeding in reeds by the water.

Grey Heron fishing on the edge of the pond.

Mallard dabbling on the surface.

Mute Swan fishing with head and neck under water.

Watch how different kinds of birds feed on your local pond. Which birds up-end the most? Which dabble the most? Which dive the most? Why is it do you think that some kinds feed differently from others?

Taking off and landing

Goldeneye

Most water birds are heavy and must work hard to get up speed for their take-off. Many of them run over the surface, flapping their wings until they are going fast enough to become airborne. Coming in to land, they fly low over the water, with their feet sticking out. These act as a brake when they touch down on the surface.

Gull

Moulting

Mallards moult in late summer. The male loses his colourful feathers and becomes a mottled brown all over. For a time he looks rather like the female. New bright-coloured feathers grow by early winter.

When danger threatens Mallard ducklings, the mother stretches out her neck and quacks loudly. The ducklings dive to escape.

Woodlands and forests

Woodlands and forests are good places to spot birds, but you will see them more easily in places that are not too dark. Woods with open spaces are lighter and have more plants and insects for birds to eat.

Woods with broad-leaved trees, such as oak and beech, contain many more birds than old pine forests, which can be very dark. But old pine forests can have special birds, such as Capercaillies, that can be found nowhere else.

The **Nightingale** (16.5 cm) can often be heard singing in woods and forests, but is rarely seen. It builds its nest among trees and bushes close to the ground.

The **Goldcrest** (9 cm) is the smallest European bird. It is often found in coniferous or mixed woods all year round.

The **Coal Tit** (11.5 cm) is the same size as a Blue Tit. It nests in coniferous forests.

The **Chaffinch** (15 cm) is a common bird, often found in broad-leaved woodlands and coniferous woods. In winter it prefers to live in open land.

The sizes given are beak-to-tail measurements.

If it is windy, watch out for falling branches in the woods. Try not to stand or sit near trees which have nests in them. You might frighten away the parent birds.

The **Chiffchaff** (11 cm) is smaller than a sparrow and visits Europe from Africa during the summer. It is often found in broad-leaved woods and in young pine plantations.

The food of woodland birds

The Tawny Owl feeds on small animals. Its eyesight and hearing are very good.

In autumn, Jays collect acorns. They bury many of them and then dig them up when they need food.

Many birds, such as the Garden Warbler here, feed on caterpillars.

The Pied Fly Catcher swoops down on insects from a look-out branch.

Special beaks

Some birds, such as the Hawfinch and the Crossbill, have special beaks for eating seeds.

Jay

Hawfinch   **Crossbill**

The **Black Woodpecker** (46 cm) is the largest European woodpecker. It is found mainly in coniferous forests in many parts of Europe, but not in Britain.

Holes in trees

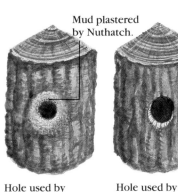

Mud plastered by Nuthatch.

Hole used by a Nuthatch.

Hole used by a woodpecker.

Woodpecker holes

4 cm
Lesser
Spotted

4.5 cm
Great
Spotted

6.5 cm
Green

10 cm
Black

The different kinds of woodpecker all make nesting holes in trees. These are sometimes used by other birds, such as the Nuthatch, or even bats and dormice.

The **Nuthatch** (14 cm) feeds on nuts from hazel, beech and oak trees.

The **Green Woodpecker** (32 cm) is the same size as a pigeon. It is frequently seen on the ground, feeding on ants, and is usually found in broad-leaved woodlands.

The **Woodcock** (34 cm) is found in broad-leaved woodlands where its plumage blends in perfectly with the dead leaves on the ground. It has a long, thin beak.

The **Lesser Spotted Woodpecker** (14.5 cm) is the smallest European woodpecker. It is found in broad-leaved woods. The male bird has a bright red crown.

Woodlands at night

There are many different kinds of owl living in woods. They range in size from the small Pygmy Owl, which is only 16.5 cm high, to the much bigger Eagle Owl, which can be as large as 71 cm.

These four owls are all drawn to the same scale.

The Nightjar sleeps during the day, so is rarely seen. Its song can be heard after dark in summer.

These three owls are all drawn to the same scale.

Pygmy Owl

Scops Owl

Little Owl

Little Owl

Long-eared Owl

Tawny Owl

Eagle Owl

Nightjar

Towns and cities

Bird spotting in towns and cities can be just as rewarding as in the countryside. In densely built up areas, you may only see Pigeons, Starlings and House Sparrows. Where there are gardens and parks you will find many other kinds of birds.

Some of these birds are quite used to people and can be very tame. You may even be able to get quite close to them and tempt them to feed from your hand. The pictures here show some of the most common birds in towns and cities.

The **Kestrel** is a town as well as a country bird. The town Kestrel usually feeds on sparrows, and nests high up on the tops of buildings.

Cliff birds that live in towns

Black Redstart

Black Redstarts once nested on sea-cliffs and rocks. Now you are more likely to find them in towns. They make their nests on buildings.

The **Long-tailed Tit** is a hedge bird that can often be seen in parks and gardens. In autumn and winter, family groups of about a dozen gather together.

The **Black-headed Gull** is one of the commonest town gulls. You will often see large numbers of them near reservoirs and gravel pits and in large grassy areas.

You will never see a **Swift** on the ground or on a wire. It feeds and even sleeps on the wing. At dusk, Swifts circle high above the rooftops.

You will sometimes hear the warbling song of the **Skylark** as it flies above parks and wasteland. In winter, you may see flocks around gravel pits and reservoirs.

1
Towns and cities are surprisingly good places to look for birds. Birds need food and a place to rest and sleep. Most gardens (3) and parks (2) have

2
some trees and bushes where birds can nest and sleep without being disturbed by people. Many birds find perching places on buildings (5). Gulls fly out to

3
sleep at gravel pits (1) or reservoirs (4). Everywhere people spill or leave food which birds can eat. On the edge of town, birds find lots of food at sewage

Rock Dove   **Pigeons**

Starling

The town Pigeon is a relation of the Rock Dove, which nests on sea-cliffs. The town Pigeon is now much more common than the Rock Dove and is often very tame. It feeds on bread and any other scraps it finds in parks or in the streets, and can be a nuisance in city centres.

Starlings are one of the most common city birds. They are usually found in huge, noisy flocks.

House Martins build their mud nests under the roofs of many town houses.

White patch only on House Martin.

Swallows look rather like House Martins, but have longer tail feathers. You can often see them catching flies over rivers, gravel pits and reservoirs.

Carrion Crows are quite common in parks and gardens.

Magpies are large black and white birds and are common in parks and gardens. They use twigs to build their nests in tress and tall hedges.

4

works (4) and rubbish dumps (1). Railway sidings and canals (6), where food supplies are unloaded and often spilt, are also good feeding spots for

5

birds, and have fewer people to disturb them. Many birds eat the seeds of weeds growing on waste ground and building sites. In winter, when there is

6

little food in the countryside, many birds fly to the towns and cities. There many people put out food specially for the birds.

Sea coasts

The coast is always a good place to spot birds. In summer, many birds fly from Africa and the Antarctic to breed on European coasts. In winter, small wading birds, such as the Knot, come from the north to feed and wait for spring.

Most of the cliff-nesting birds spend the winter far out at sea. Every year many birds lose their eggs and babies because people tread on the nests or stop the parent birds from feeding the young by frightening them away.

Waders' beaks

Birds can find much food on the beach. The shape of a wading bird's beak depends on the sort of food it eats. You can try to find out what the birds are eating by digging up the sand and looking for the food in it.

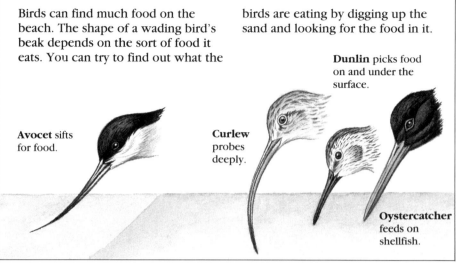

Avocet sifts for food.

Curlew probes deeply.

Dunlin picks food on and under the surface.

Oystercatcher feeds on shellfish.

Nesting places

In winter, cliffs are almost deserted, but during the breeding season, they are like large bird cities. The whole cliff is used for nesting. Each type of bird has its favourite spot for nesting.

The **Brent Goose** is a rare winter visitor from Greenland and northern Russia where it breeds. It feeds on a plant called Eelgrass, which grows only on mudflats.

Brent Goose

Knot
(summer plumage)

In winter, large flocks of **Knots** fly south from their northern breeding grounds. They feed on sandy or muddy shores. In winter, their plumage is grey.

Shelduck

The **Shelduck** is one of the most common large birds you will see on a salt marsh. Sometimes it builds its nest in an old rabbit burrow.

The **Common Tern** breeds on salt marshes, shingle or sandy shores. It builds its nest in a hollow in the ground.

Common tern

Salt marsh

Sandy shore

Shingle beach

Fish-eaters' beaks

Fish-eating birds do not all have the same kind of beak. The shape of the beak depends on the size and type of fish that the bird eats.

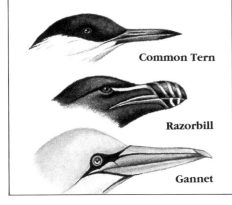

Common Tern

Razorbill

Gannet

Gannets make their nests on cliff tops. Gannets nest in large numbers and build their untidy nests about one metre apart from each other.

Puffins use their bills for digging nesting burrows in the cliff top soil. They clear away the soil with their feet.

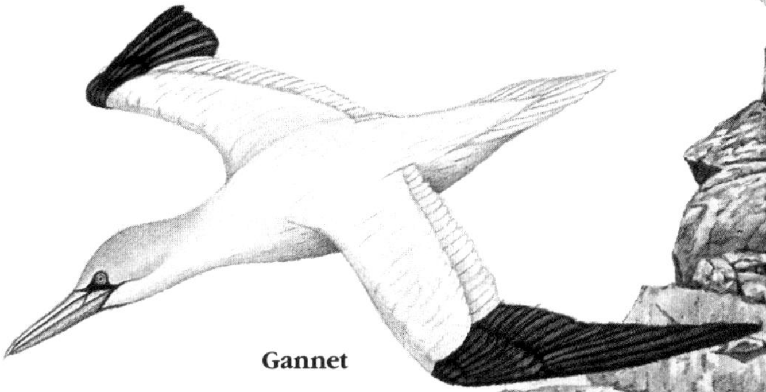

Puffin

Gannet

The **Fulmar** is a large bird that spends most of its time out at sea. It looks rather like a gull, but holds its wings straighter and stiffer when it is flying.

The **Razorbill** lays its one egg in a crack in the cliff or under a rock. The nest is sometimes a few pieces of seaweed, but often there is no proper nest at all.

Razorbill

Fulmar

The **Guillemot** makes no nest. It lays a single pear-shaped egg on a rock ledge. The shape of the egg stops it rolling off. They nest in large numbers.

Guillemot

Shag

Cormorant

The **Shag** is smaller than the Cormorant and does not have the Cormorant's white face. In the breeding season, it grows a little curly crest.

The **Cormorant's** feathers are not waterproof, so you will often see it standing on a rock or post holding out its wings to dry.

Cliffs

25

Moors and mountains

Many of the birds that live on moors and on mountains are well known because they are game-birds, such as Grouse. There are also large and powerful birds of prey, such as the Golden Eagle or Buzzard. You will see fewer birds in these places than at the coast or in woods because there is less food for them to eat. The smaller birds eat bilberries, young shoots of heather and seeds from mosses and grasses. The large birds of prey feed mainly on small birds and other animals.

Every year people get lost on moors and mountains. Make sure it is not you. Never go on your own and always tell someone where you are going. Keep to paths and wear warm clothes.

The birds and mammals on these pages are not drawn to scale.

The **Golden Eagle** is the largest bird that is found on moors and mountains. It is very rare in most parts of Europe.

The **Short-eared Owl** nests on the ground. It often hunts in the daytime and feeds on small animals, such as voles and lemmings.

These two birds look different, but are in fact very closely related. The **Red Grouse** is only found in Britain and the **Willow Grouse** only in Europe. The Willow Grouse is shown here in part of its winter plumage.

The **Buzzard** is one of the most common of the large birds of prey. It is similar to the Golden Eagle, but is smaller and stubbier.

The **Meadow Pipit** is the most common small bird that you see on moorland. It feeds on insects.

Red Grouse

Willow Grouse

Lemming

Changing colour with the seasons

Ptarmigan in summer

Ptarmigan in winter

The Ptarmigan can hide from its enemies because it always looks the same colour as the countryside. In summer, its coat is mainly brown. In winter it turns white. It lives in the mountains of northern Europe.

Shrikes

Shrikes (also known as Butcher Birds) have a habit of pinning insects, mice, lizards and even small birds onto branches or barbed wire. These food "stores" come in handy when fresh food is scarce. The Red-backed Shrike is a rare summer visitor. The Great Grey Shrike breeds in northern Europe and flies south in the winter. They can be seen in hedges, bushes, trees and on wires.

Red-backed Shrike

Great Grey Shrike

Beetle

The **Black Grouse** lives on the borders of moorland. The male (blackcock) has curved tail feathers.

The **Raven** is the largest of the Crow family. It is as big as the Buzzard. The Raven flies slowly but powerfully, and sometimes tumbles through the air.

The **Golden Plover** usually breeds on moors and hills. It lays its four eggs in a nest on the ground.

The **Wheatear** builds its nest in holes in walls and in old rabbit burrows.

The **Dipper** lives by mountain streams. It feeds on insects it catches under water.

The **Ring Ouzel** is a relative of the Blackbird and lives in remote mountain valleys and on moors.

Short-tailed vole

25

Migrating birds

Every year millions of birds move from one part of the world to another. This is called migration. Many birds come to Europe from southern Africa in April and May. During the southern African winter, which falls in June, July and August, there is not enough food for birds, such as Swallows.

Swallows fly north to breed in Europe where there is enough food. In late August and September they fly south where the summer is just starting. Again, the reason for this migration is to find good supplies of food.

Keep a record of migrant birds. Note down the first and last dates you see them. Also keep a record of the weather in spring and autumn. Does this have an affect on the dates when birds arrive or leave?

April 22nd
Weather warm and dry. First swallows arrive from the south.

The Swallow

1 Swallows spend the winter months in southern Africa, but in March huge flocks start to move northwards to Europe. They come here to breed.

2 There is very little water in the desert, so the Swallows fly across it without stopping. They live off the food and water which they have stored as fat under their skin.

3 One of the most dangerous parts of the journey is crossing the Mediterranean Sea. Many Swallows take the shortest route, across the Straits of Gibraltar.

4 By the end of May most Swallows have arrived and built their nests. In late summer they get ready for the long journey back to southern Africa.

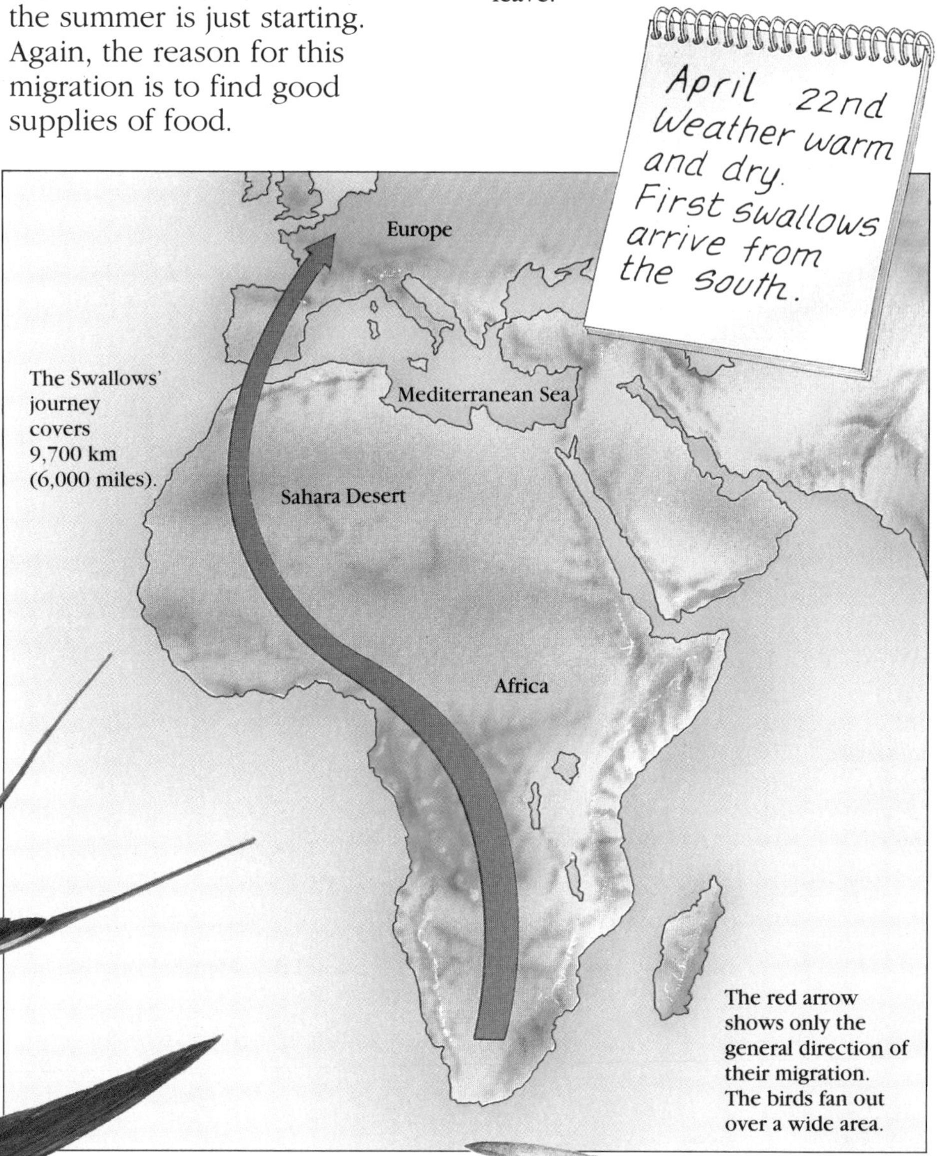

The Swallows' journey covers 9,700 km (6,000 miles).

Europe

Mediterranean Sea

Sahara Desert

Africa

The red arrow shows only the general direction of their migration. The birds fan out over a wide area.

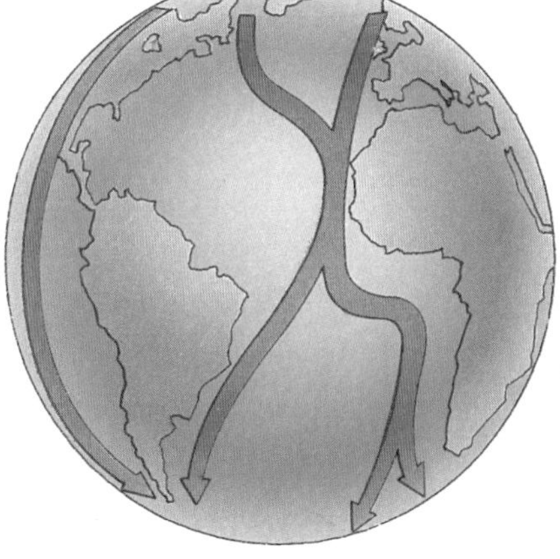

Arctic Tern

Some birds fly even longer distances than the Swallow. One of these is the Arctic Tern. It breeds in the Arctic and then flies south, all the way to the southern tip of South America and southern Africa. During the journey it stays mostly out at sea. These birds nest in large flocks, called terneries. The Arctic Tern shown here is in its summer colour. In autumn, the forehead is white and the bill and legs are blackish.

Arctic

In some places in Europe, flocks of birds, such as White Storks, can be spotted waiting by the coast for good weather, so they can continue their migration across the sea.

The Redwing is a member of the Thrush family and looks like the Song Thrush but has pink on its sides. It is a winter visitor to Europe, coming from the north and travelling in large flocks.

The Hoopoe, with its parrot-like crest and floppy flight, does not seem capable of flying far, but every autumn it flies to Africa from Europe and makes a return journey in spring.

White Stork

Redwing

Summer visitors
The Blackcap and the Willow Warbler both belong to the warbler family and are two of the most common summer visitors to Europe. They come from Africa. In winter a few Blackcaps stay in Europe.

Willow Warbler

Blackcap

Hoopoe

Starling

Many Starlings fly south in winter and are attracted to bright lights at night, such as lighthouses. Many of them are killed by flying into buildings where they see lights. Starlings are one of the most common birds in towns and cities.

27

Identifying birds by size

Sparrow-sized birds

The notes for each bird give size from beak to tail. Each panel has birds of a similar size. The dots beside each bird tell you where to look for it.

The birds inside this panel are all drawn to the same scale.

- **Water**
- **Woods**
- **Towns and gardens**
- **Fields**

Wren. 9 cm. Smallest bird you will see in gardens. Holds its tail cocked over its back.

Goldcrest. 9 cm. Smallest European bird. Feeds on insects and spiders.

Blue Tit. 11.5 cm. Only tit with blue head and wings. One of the most common garden birds.

Treecreeper. 12.5 cm. This mouse-like bird climbs trees.

Nuthatch. 14 cm. Has a sharp straight bill used for cracking open nuts.

Long-tailed Tit. 14 cm. Tail very long. Often seen in small flocks.

Great Tit. 14 cm. Has a black band down its belly.

Coal Tit. 11.5 cm. Has a white stripe on its neck.

Sand Martin. 12 cm. Has brown back and collar. Nests in holes in banks.

House Martin. 12.5 cm. Has a white rump and a shorter tail than the Swallow. Often nests in large flocks.

Swallow. 19 cm. Has long tail feathers and a dark throat. Feeds on insects.

Swift. 16.5 cm. Has very long curved wings.

Blackbird-sized birds

The birds inside this panel are all drawn to the same scale.

Adult   Female   Male

Juvenile

Starling. 21.5 cm. On the ground has an upright waddling walk. This common bird is often seen in large flocks.

Blackbird. 25 cm. The male is all black with an orange beak. The female and young are brown with a brown beak.

Song Thrush. 23 cm. Both sexes look the same, with a brown back and spotted breast. Often feeds on snails.

Mistle Thrush. 27 cm. A greyer bird than the Song Thrush and the spots on the breast are larger and closer together.

Remember - if you cannot see a picture of the bird you want to identify on these pages, turn to the pages earlier in this section which show birds that live in the sort of place where you saw your bird. Pages 6 and 32-33, which show bird shapes in flight, will help you too.

Adult   Juvenile   Female   Female

Male   Male

Robin. 14 cm. Can be very tame. Has an orange breast.

Bullfinch. 14.5-16 cm. Has a black cap and white rump.

Greenfinch. 14.5 cm. Has yellow wing bars and a greenish rump.

Goldfinch. 12 cm. Has a red face and a black and white head.

Male   Female   Male   Female

Dunnock. 14.5 cm. Feeds on the ground and moves slowly with a kind of creeping walk.

House Sparrow. 14.5 cm. The male has a grey and brown head and black throat.

Tree Sparrow. 14 cm. Has a brown cap and a black spot on its white cheeks.

Chaffinch. 15 cm. Has white wing bars and white outer tail feathers.

Pied Wagtail   White Wagtail   Male   Female   Male

Female

Kingfisher. 16.5 cm. Catches small fish, shellfish and tadpoles for food.

The **Pied Wagtail** (18 cm) lives in Britain, the **White** (18 cm) in Europe.

Skylark. 18 cm. Has white outer tail feathers.

Yellowhammer. 16.5 cm. The male has a yellow head.

Linnet. 13.5 cm. The male has a red forehead and chest.

Adult   Juvenile   Adult   Male   Female

Juvenile

Great Spotted Woodpecker. 23 cm. Has large white wing patches and a black line from beak to neck.

Green Woodpecker. 32 cm. Has a bright red head and yellow rump. Often feeds on ants on the ground.

Cuckoo. 33 cm. Has a long tail. It lays its eggs in the nests of other birds.

Kestrel. 34 cm. The most common falcon. Often hovers before dropping on its prey.

29

Remember - if you cannot see a picture of the bird you want to identify on these pages, turn to the pages earlier in this section which show birds that live in the sort of place where you saw your bird. Pages 6 and 32-33, which show bird shapes in flight, will help you too.

Crow-sized birds

The birds inside this panel are all drawn to scale.

Collared Dove. 32 cm. Has a black half collar at the back of the neck.

Woodpigeon. 41 cm. Has a white patch on each side of the neck.

Buzzard. 51-56 cm. Has broad wings and tail. Plumage is dark brown and cream.

Barn Owl. 34 cm. A large white-looking owl. It hunts in twilight or at night. The remains of meals can be found as pellets.

Lapwing. 30 cm. Has a thin crest and broad, black and white wings which show up when it is flying.

Herring Gull. 56-66 cm. Commonest gull on the coast. Has a large yellow beak with a red spot near the tip and grey wings.

Black-headed Gull. 35-38 cm. In winter, instead of a dark head, it has only a dark mark behind the eyes.

Mallard-sized birds

The birds inside this panel are all drawn to scale.

Breeding plumage (spring and summer)

Non-breeding plumage (winter)

Coot. 38 cm. Larger than a Moorhen. Is all black with a white beak and forehead. Likes large open stretches of water.

Moorhen. 33 cm. Its beak is red and the underside of its tail white. Swims with a jerky movement.

Great Crested Grebe. 48 cm. The largest grebe. In summer, it has brownish frills round the neck. In winter, it has blackish ear tufts.

Female

Male

Female

Male

Tufted Duck. 43 cm. The most common diving duck. The male has a long drooping crest, the female is browner with a much smaller crest. They form large flocks on lakes and reservoirs.

Mallard. 58 cm. The male has a green head, white collar and purple-brown breast. Both birds have a blue patch and white bars on their wings, which show up best when they are flying.

30

Jackdaw. 33 cm. Has a grey head and is smaller than the all-black crows.

Magpie. 46 cm. A large bird with a long tail and black and white plumage.

Carrion

Hooded

The northern form of the **Carrion Crow** (47 cm) has some grey feathers. It is called the **Hooded Crow** (47 cm).

Rook. 46 cm. Has a thinner beak than the crow, with a bare white face and "baggy trousers".

Curlew. 51-58 cm. Largest wader. Has a long downward curved beak, a brown body and long legs.

Male

Female

Pheasant. Male 66-89 cm. Female 53-63 cm. A large game-bird. The male is brightly coloured, the female browner with a shorter tail.

Large water birds

These birds are NOT drawn to the same scale.

Whooper Swan

Bewick's Swan

Female Mute Swan

Juvenile Mute Swan

Male Mute Swan

Grey Heron. 90 cm. A large grey bird, often seen standing at the water's edge. The nest is usually built in a tree.

Cormorant. 90 cm. This sea bird has a white chin and cheeks. Often seen sitting on rocks with its wings half open.

Mute Swan. 152 cm. Has an orange bill with a black knob at the base. Swims with its neck curved.

Bewick's and Whooper Swan. 122 cm and 152 cm. Bewick's has a shorter bill with a small yellow patch. Both hold their necks stiffly when swimming. They are winter visitors.

Birds in flight

Here are some illustrations
to help you identify
birds in flight. The sizes
given are beak-to-tail
measurements.

Wheatear
15cm.

Lapwing
30cm.

Kestral
34cm.

Short-eared
Owl. 38cm.

Peregrine
Falcon 42cm.

Woodpigeon
41cm.

Oystercatcher
43cm.

Avocet
43cm.

Hen Harrier
47cm.

Goshawk
55cm.

Osprey
54cm.

Buzzard
54cm.

Black Kite
54cm.

Herring Gull
60cm.

Mallard
58cm.

White-tailed
Eagle 69-91cm.

Greylag goose
76-89.

White Stork
102cm.

Pheasant
66-89.

Mute Swan
152cm.

33

Trees are everywhere. Only deserts and the tops of mountains are without them. This part of the book tells you about trees and how to study them. It shows you the different parts of a tree, how they work and how they can help you to identify the tree.

It tells the whole story of a tree, from the moment a seed sprouts to when a mature tree dies or is cut down for timber. There are also special tips on how to collect information and specimens.

If you want to identify a tree, look first at pages 60 to 63, called *Common trees you can spot*. If you fail to find a picture of your tree there, turn to the pages that deal with the part of the tree you are looking at, such as a leaf or a piece of the bark.

TREES & LEAVES

Contents

How a tree grows

This is the life story of a Sycamore, but all trees grow in a similar way. Although there are many different kinds of trees, they all sprout from seeds, grow larger, have flowers, form fruits and shed seeds.

You can study many of these steps in a tree's life. You can watch a tiny seedling sprout and then keep a record of its growth. You can count the girdle scars on a young tree to find out its age.

Older trees have flowers and fruits, although they may be hard to see on some trees. Not all trees have flowers as large as the Horse Chestnut's or fruits as big as the Apple tree's. Most fruits ripen in autumn, but some appear in early summer and spring.

An important part of a tree that you do not usually see is the roots. If you find an overturned tree, look at the roots and try to measure them. Look also at logs and tree stumps for the layers of wood and bark. They can tell you the age of the tree and how quickly it has grown.

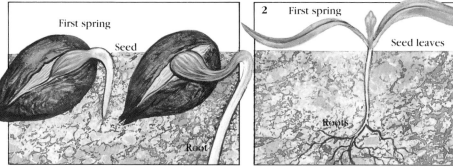

The tree starts growing in spring from a seed which has been lying in the soil all winter. At this time, with the help of the food stored inside it, the seed sends down a root into the soil to suck up water and minerals.

Next, the seed sends up a tiny shoot which pokes above the ground and into the light. Two fleshy seed leaves open up with a small bud between them. These leaves are not the same shape as the tree's real leaves will be.

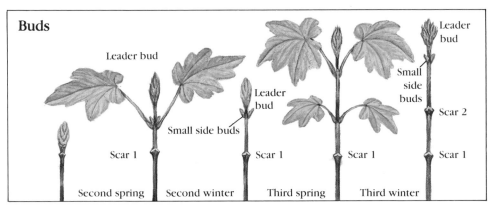

Buds

In the second spring, the bud opens and there are two new leaves. A new shoot grows too, with another bud at the tip. In autumn, the leaves drop off. Every year the same thing happens, and every time the leaves fall off, they leave a girdle scar on the stem. Buds on the sides of the stem also grow shoots, but they do not grow as fast as the leader shoot at the top of the tree. Each year the tree grows taller, and the roots grow deeper.

Pollen on the flowers

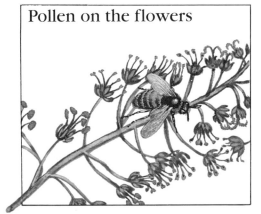

When the tree is about twelve years old, it grows flowers on its branches in the spring. Bees and other insects, searching for nectar, visit the flowers and some of the pollen from the flowers sticks on to their hairy bodies.

Fruits

When the bees visit other flowers from the same tree, some of the pollen on their bodies rubs off on to the female parts of the flowers. When the pollen and female parts are joined, the flowers are fertilized and become fruits.

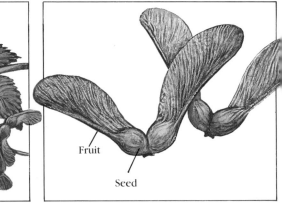

Later that year, the fruits fall off the tree. The Sycamore fruits here spin like tiny helicopters, carrying the seeds away from the parent tree. The wings rot on the ground, and the seeds are ready to grow the following spring.

3 Leaves
Seed leaves
First summer

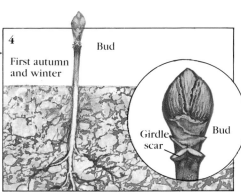

4 First autumn and winter
Bud
Girdle scar
Bud

Holly leaf

The seed leaves have stored food in them to help the seedling grow. Soon the bud opens, and the first pair of real leaves appears. These will trap light from the sun to grow more food. The seed leaves then drop off. The roots grow longer.

In the autumn, all the leaves change colour and drop off, leaving a "girdle scar" around the stem where they were attached. A bud is left at the end of the shoot. The bud does not grow during the winter. It stays dormant.

Many broadleaved trees are deciduous, which means that they lose their leaves in autumn. They do this because their leaves cannot work properly in cold weather, and there is not enough sunlight in winter for the leaves to make food for the tree.

Most conifers are evergreens. Their needles are tougher than most broadleaves, and they can keep making food even in the dark of winter.

A few broadleaved trees, such as Holly, are also evergreen. Like conifer needles, their leaves have a waxy coating which helps them survive the winter.

Inside a tree

Each year, a tree grows more branches. The trunk thickens by adding a new layer of wood to hold the branches up, and the roots grow deeper and wider. This picture shows you the inside of the trunk, and all its different parts.

1 Heartwood. This is old sapwood which is dead and has become very hard. It makes the tree strong and rigid.

2 Rays. In a cross-section of a log you can see pale lines. These are called rays and they carry food sideways.

3 Cambium. This layer is so thin that you can hardly see it. Its job is to make a new layer of sapwood (see page 20) each year. This makes the trunk thicker and stronger.

4 Sapwood. This layer also has tiny tubes in it which carry the sap (water and minerals) to all parts of the tree from the roots. Each year a new ring of this wood is made by the cambium.

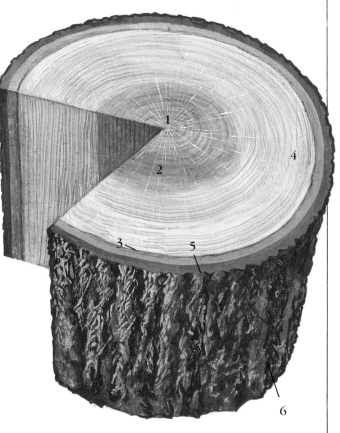

5 Phloem. Just inside the bark are tubes which carry food down from the leaves to all parts of the tree, including the roots.

6 Bark is the outer layer which protects the tree from sun, rain and fungi which might attack it.

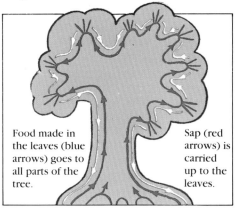

Food made in the leaves (blue arrows) goes to all parts of the tree.

Sap (red arrows) is carried up to the leaves.

To help it grow, the tree makes food for itself in the leaves, which contain a green chemical called chlorophyll. In sunlight, the chlorophyll can change oxygen from the air, water, and minerals brought up from the soil into food for the tree. If a tree gets no light to make food it will die.

Scots Pine cone

Seeds fall out of cone.

Some trees, such as the Scots Pine, have fruits called cones, which stay on the tree, but open up to let the seeds fall out by themselves. When the cones are old and dried up, they usually fall off the tree too.

How to identify trees

One of the best ways of identifying a tree is to look at its leaves. Be careful though, because some trees have leaves that are very similar. For example, a London Plane leaf could be confused with a Norway Maple leaf. So when you have named your tree just by identifying a leaf, always check that you are correct by looking at other parts of the tree, such as the flowers or bark.

Trees can be divided into three groups: broadleaved, coniferous, and palm trees (see the pictures to the right here). Try to decide which group your tree belongs to. There is something to give you clues in every season of the year. In spring and summer, look at the leaves and flowers. In autumn, look at the fruits. Winter is the best time to study buds, twigs, bark and tree shapes.

You do not need to go into a woodland or forest to study trees. Look at the many different kinds that grow in gardens, parks and roads. Sometimes you can find rare trees in gardens.

Broadleaved trees

Lime (winter)

English Oak (summer)

Common Beech (spring)

Beech leaf and flower

Japanese Maple (autumn)

Most broadleaved trees have wide, flat leaves which they drop in winter. Some broadleaved trees, though, such as Holly, Laurel, Holm Oak and Box, are evergreen and keep their leaves in winter.

Broadleaved trees have seeds that are encased in fruits. The timber of broadleaved trees is called hardwood, because it is usually harder than the wood of most conifers, or softwood trees.

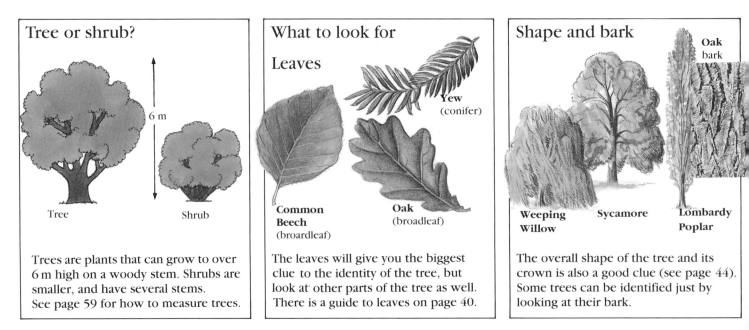

Tree or shrub?

6 m

Tree

Shrub

Trees are plants that can grow to over 6 m high on a woody stem. Shrubs are smaller, and have several stems. See page 59 for how to measure trees.

What to look for

Leaves

Yew (conifer)

Common Beech (broardleaf)

Oak (broadleaf)

The leaves will give you the biggest clue to the identity of the tree, but look at other parts of the tree as well. There is a guide to leaves on page 40.

Shape and bark

Oak bark

Weeping Willow

Sycamore

Lombardy Poplar

The overall shape of the tree and its crown is also a good clue (see page 44). Some trees can be identified just by looking at their bark.

Conifers

Scots Pine

Cone and needles

Norway Spruce

European Larch (in winter)

European Larch (in summer)

Palms

Leaf

Canary Palm

Most conifers have narrow, needle-like or scaly leaves, and are evergreen, that is they keep their leaves in winter. The Larch is one conifer that is not evergreen, as the tree loses its leaves in winter.

Conifer fruits are usually woody cones, but some conifers, such as the Yew, have berry-like fruits. The overall shape of conifers is more regular and symmetrical than the shape of most broadleaved trees.

Palms have trunks that have no branches. They look like giant stalks. The leaves grow from the top of the tree. Unlike other trees, palms grows taller without getting thicker.

Winter buds

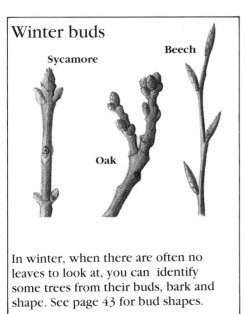

Sycamore

Beech

Oak

In winter, when there are often no leaves to look at, you can identify some trees from their buds, bark and shape. See page 43 for bud shapes.

Flowers

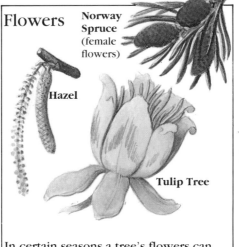

Norway Spruce (female flowers)

Hazel

Tulip Tree

In certain seasons a tree's flowers can help you to identify it. But some trees do not flower every year. For tree flowers, see pages 46-47.

Fruits and seeds

Horse Chestnut fruit

Scots Pine cone

All trees have fruits bearing seeds which may grow into new trees. This Horse Chestnut conker and the pine cone are both fruits. See pages 48-49.

Leaves

One of the things that most people notice about a tree is its leaves. A big Oak tree has more than 250,000 leaves and a conifer tree may have many millions of needles.

The leaves fan out to catch as much sunlight as possible. With the green chlorophyll inside them, they make food for the tree. They take in gases from the air through tiny holes, and give out water vapour and gases in the same way. Once the food is made, it is carried through veins to other parts of the leaf. The veins make the leaf strong like a skeleton.

The leaf stem carries water from the twig and also helps the leaf to move into the light. It is tough so that the leaf does not break off in strong winds.

The leaves of broadleaved trees and conifers look different, but they do the same work. Most conifer leaves can survive the winter, but the leaves of most broadleaves fall off in the autumn. A conifer needle stays on a tree for about three to five years.

Tracking down your mystery leaf

1. Decide if the leaf is from a conifer or a broadleaved tree.

2. Look at its shape and its edge.

3. Notice the way the leaves are arranged on the twig.

4. Look at the colour and leaf surface.

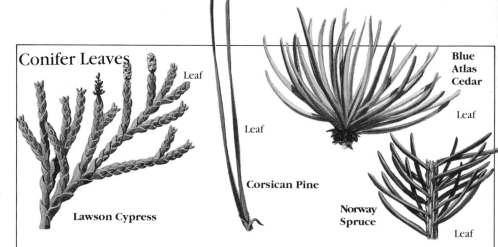

Conifer Leaves

Lawson Cypress

Corsican Pine

Blue Atlas Cedar

Norway Spruce

Leaf

Here you can see three types of conifer leaf. Many conifers have narrow needle-like leaves which are either single, in small bunches or in clusters. They can be very sharp and spiky. But other conifers, such as the Cypresses, have tiny scale-like leaves, overlaping one another.

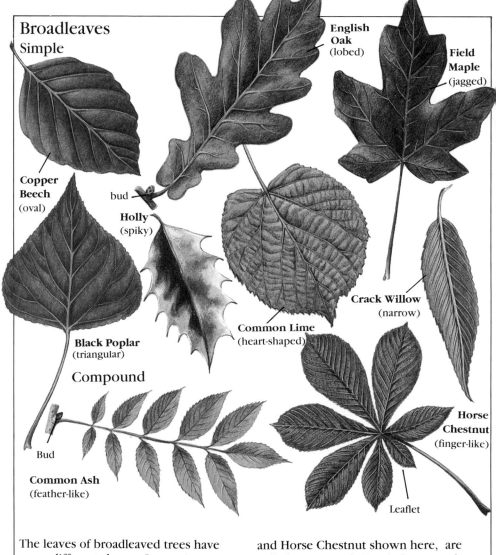

Broadleaves
Simple

Copper Beech (oval)

bud

Holly (spiky)

Black Poplar (triangular)

English Oak (lobed)

Field Maple (jagged)

Common Lime (heart-shaped)

Crack Willow (narrow)

Compound

Bud

Common Ash (feather-like)

Horse Chestnut (finger-like)

Leaflet

The leaves of broadleaved trees have many different shapes. Leaves in one piece are called simple. Those made up of many leaflets, such as Common Ash and Horse Chestnut shown here, are called compound. Simple leaves and compound leaves both have one bud at the base of their stems.

40

These leaves are not drawn to the same scale.

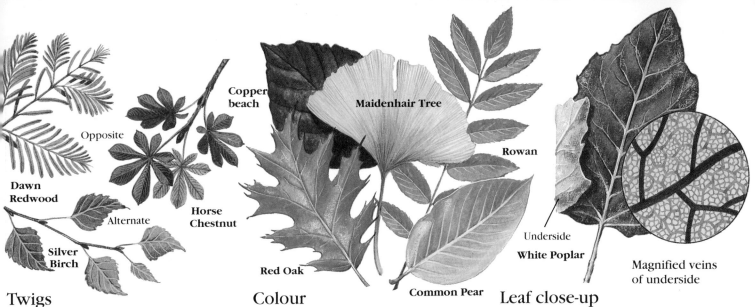

Twigs

Leaves are arranged on twigs in various ways. They can be opposite each other in pairs, or they can be single and alternate from one side of the twig to the other.

Colour

Leaves are green because of the chlorophyll inside them. In autumn, the chlorophyll in broadleaves decays. They change colour before they fall.

Leaf close-up

Leaves have a network of tiny veins. Their upper surface is tough and often glossy, to stop the sun from drying them out. The underside is often hairy.

Leaf scrapbook

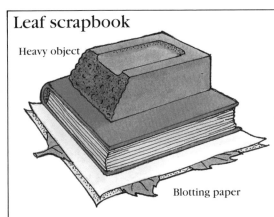

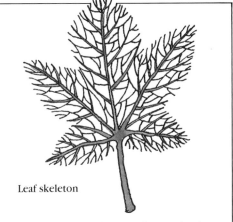

Leaf skeleton

Keep a scrapbook of the leaves you find. Place each leaf between two sheets of blotting paper. Then put a book and a heavy object on top.

Leave them for about a week. When the leaves are flat and dry, mount them in a scrapbook with sticky tape. Label the leaves and write down where and

when you found them. When a dead leaf has crumbled, the strong stem and veins remain as a skeleton. You will often find these in winter.

Leaf tiles

Press the leaf on to the "clay" with a rolling pin.

The finished tile can be painted or varnished.

Make your clay by mixing together:
2 cups flour (not self-raising)
1 cup salt
1 cup water
2 tablespoons cooking oil

Scatter some flour onto a surface top and shape your "clay" into a ball. Roll it out flat with a floured rolling pin, until it is about 2 cm thick. Press your leaf, vein side down, onto the clay so that it

leaves a mark. Remove the leaf and bake the clay in the oven at 150°C (250°F) for about two hours. When the tile has cooled, you can paint it or varnish it.

Winter buds

Most broadleaved trees have no leaves in winter, but you can still identify them by their winter buds. These contain the beginnings of a shoot, leaves and flowers, which will appear in the next year.

The thick, overlapping bud scales protect a shoot from the cold and from attack by insects. In places where winter is the dry season, the bud scales keep a new shoot from drying out. If the tiny undeveloped leaf has no bud scales, it may be covered with furry hairs to protect it.

In spring, when it gets warmer, a new shoot swells and breaks open the protective hard scales. At the end of the growing season, each shoot will have a new winter bud at the tip. There are many buds on a twig. The leading bud, which is usually at the tip, contains the shoot which will grow most. Shoots become twigs and eventually branches.

Other buds hold leaves and flowers. They are also reserves in case the leading bud is damaged.

Inside a bud there are tiny leaves and flowers, all folded up. If you cut a bud in half and look at it through a lens, you can see the different parts.

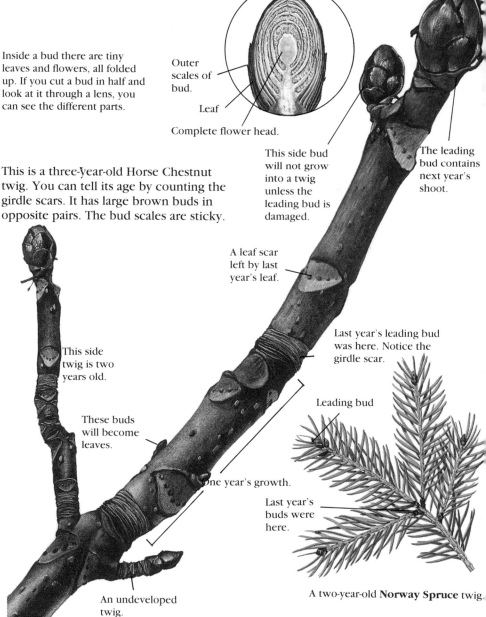

Outer scales of bud.

Leaf

Complete flower head.

This side bud will not grow into a twig unless the leading bud is damaged.

The leading bud contains next year's shoot.

This is a three-year-old Horse Chestnut twig. You can tell its age by counting the girdle scars. It has large brown buds in opposite pairs. The bud scales are sticky.

A leaf scar left by last year's leaf.

This side twig is two years old.

These buds will become leaves.

Last year's leading bud was here. Notice the girdle scar.

Leading bud

One year's growth.

Last year's buds were here.

An undeveloped twig.

A two-year-old **Norway Spruce** twig.

Forcing buds indoors

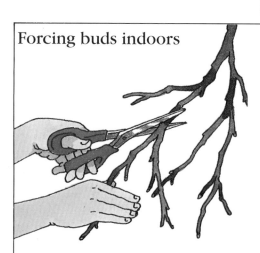

You can "force" buds to open in winter or early spring by bringing them indoors. The best ones to try are Horse Chestnut, Birch, Willow and Forsythia.

Cut the twigs with scissors. Don't break them! Always ask the owner before cutting and don't take too much. Place twigs in water in a vase or jam jar. Place

them in a sunny spot indoors, then wait for the buds to open. This may take some weeks. Draw the buds before and after they have opened.

Winter bud indentification chart

What to look for

If you try to identify trees by their winter buds, you will see that they vary a great deal. Here is a list of things to look for:

1 How are the buds positioned on the twig? Like leaves, buds can be in opposite pairs or single and alternate.

2 What colour are the buds and the twig?

3 What shape is the twig? Are the buds pointed or rounded?

4 Is the bud covered with hairs or scales? If there are scales, how many? Is the bud sticky?

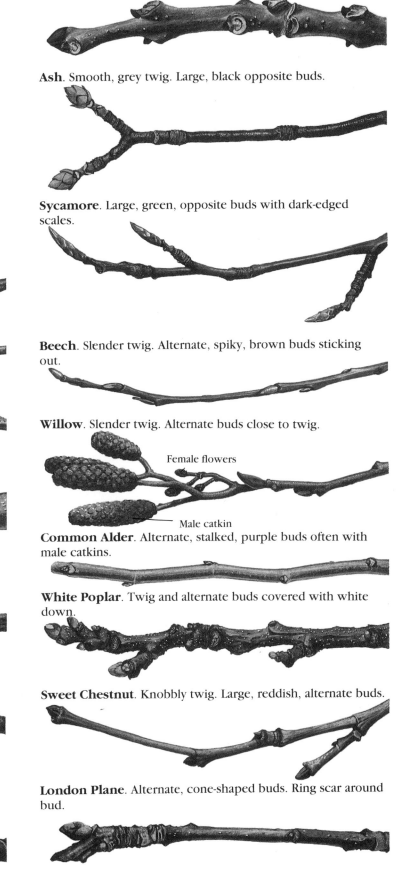

Ash. Smooth, grey twig. Large, black opposite buds.

Sycamore. Large, green, opposite buds with dark-edged scales.

Beech. Slender twig. Alternate, spiky, brown buds sticking out.

Willow. Slender twig. Alternate buds close to twig.

Female flowers

Male catkin

Common Alder. Alternate, stalked, purple buds often with male catkins.

White Poplar. Twig and alternate buds covered with white down.

Sweet Chestnut. Knobbly twig. Large, reddish, alternate buds.

London Plane. Alternate, cone-shaped buds. Ring scar around bud.

Whitebeam. Downy, green, alternate buds.

False Acacia. Grey twig. Thorns next to tiny, alternate buds.

English Elm. Zigzag twig. Alternate, blackish-red buds.

Common Lime. Zigzag twig. Alternate, reddish buds with two scales.

Walnut. Thick, hollow twig. Big, black, velvety, alternate buds.

Turkey Oak. Clusters of alternate buds with whiskers.

Wild Cherry. Large, glossy, red buds grouped at tip of twig.

Magnolia. Huge, furry, green-grey buds.

These twigs are drawn life size.

43

Shape

Look at all these different tree shapes. Each type of tree has its own typical shape made up from the arrangement and shape of its branches. Winter is the best time of year to see the shapes of broadleaved trees because their branches are not hidden by leaves.

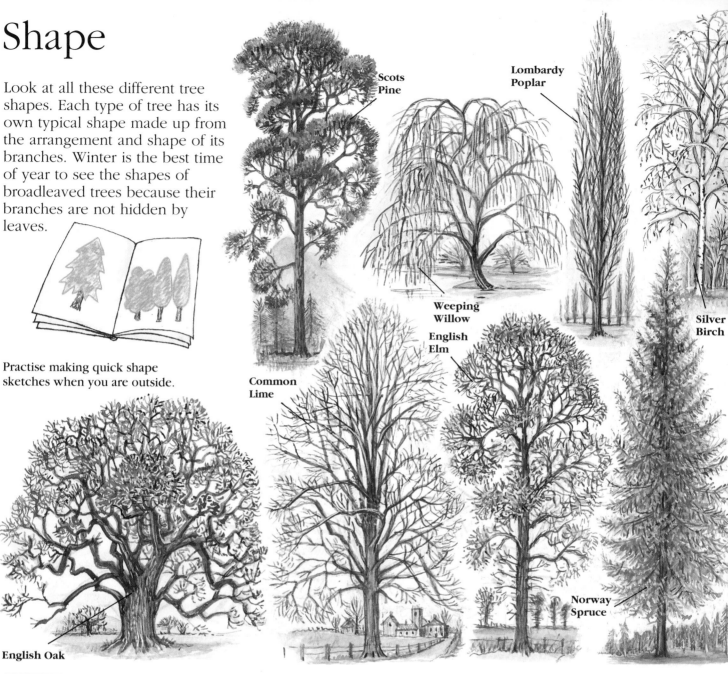

Practise making quick shape sketches when you are outside.

Scots Pine

Lombardy Poplar

Weeping Willow

English Elm

Silver Birch

Common Lime

English Oak

Norway Spruce

How trees are shaped

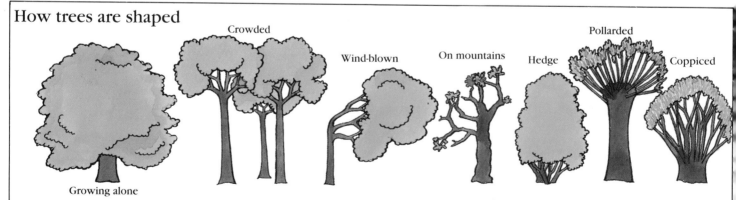

Growing alone

Crowded

Wind-blown

On mountains

Hedge

Pollarded

Coppiced

Trees grow a wide crown or top, so their leaves will get lots of sunlight. Where trees crowd together, they grow thin and tall to try and reach the light. Weather changes the shape of trees. Steady wind from one direction or salty sea winds can make trees grow bent and one-sided. On mountains, trees are dwarfed and gnarled by the cold and drying wind. Trees are also pruned or cut by man to grow in special ways. Pollarding means cutting off the branches of a tree. Coppicing is cutting the trunk down to the ground. This causes long, new shoots to grow.

Bark

The outside of the tree is covered in a hard, tough layer of bark. It protects the tree from drying out and from damage by insects or animals. It also keeps the inside of a tree at a steady temperature. Under the bark there are tubes (phloem) carrying food (sap) which can be damaged if the bark is stripped off. If this happens, the tree may die.

When the tree is young, the bark is thin and smooth, but with age it thickens and forms different patterns. You can identify trees by their bark.

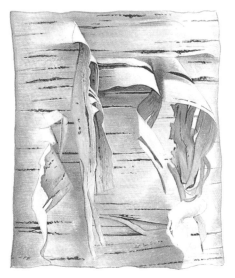

Silver Birch bark peels off in wispy strips that look like ribbons.

English Oak bark has deep ridges and cracks.

How bark patterns form

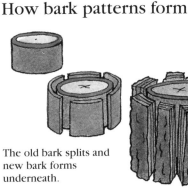

The old bark splits and new bark forms underneath.

Bark is dead and cannot grow or stretch. As wood inside the bark grows outwards, the bark splits, peels or cracks in a way that is special to each type of tree.

The bark of Scots Pine flakes off in large pieces.

Beech has smooth thin bark, which flakes off in tiny pieces.

Bark rubbings

Sticky tape

You need strong thin paper, sticky tape and wax crayons or heel-ball. Tape the paper securely to the tree. Rub firmly with the crayon, but do not tear the paper. Watch the bark pattern appear.

Candle

Rubbing that has been painted.

You can also rub the paper with candle wax. Then at home, paint over the rubbing done in this way. The bark pattern will stay the colour of the candle.

Cork

The bark of the Cork Oak is so thick that it can be removed without damaging the tree. Cork is used in many ways to keep in moisture and to resist heat. Table mats are often made from cork.

Flowers

All trees produce flowers in order to make seeds that can grow into new trees. The flowers vary from tree to tree in size, shape and colour. Some are so small that you may not notice them.

Flowers have male parts called stamens and female parts called ovaries. The stamen produces pollen, while the ovary contains ovules. When pollen from the stamen reaches the ovules in the ovary, the flower is fertilized. Fertilized flowers grow into fruits which contain seeds.

Flowers which have both ovaries and stamens, such as the Cherry, are called "perfect". On other trees the ovaries and the stamens are in different flowers. Then, the female flowers grow in separate clusters to male the flowers. The clusters can be cone shaped or long and dangling. A few trees, such as Yew, Holly and Willow, have their male and female flowers on entirely separate trees.

Parts of a flower

Petal

Stigma.

Ovary with ovules.

Stamen with pollen.

Stalk

Sepal

This is a cross-section of a Cherry blossom, which is a typical "perfect" flower as it has male and female parts.

European Larch

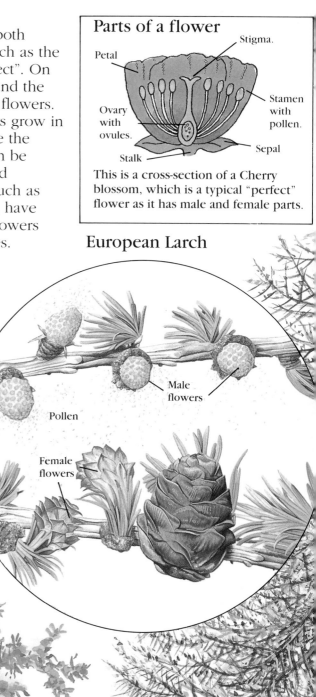

Male flowers

Pollen

Female flowers

Japanese Cherry

Stamens

Stigma

The Japanese Cherry has showy "perfect" flowers which attract insects. Although the flower has both an ovary and stamens, they ripen at different times. This stops the flower from pollinating itself. Pollination between two trees makes a healthier seed.

Like most conifers, the European Larch has separate male and female flowers on the same tree. The pollen is carried up by wind to the female flowers which grow into cones when they are fertilized.

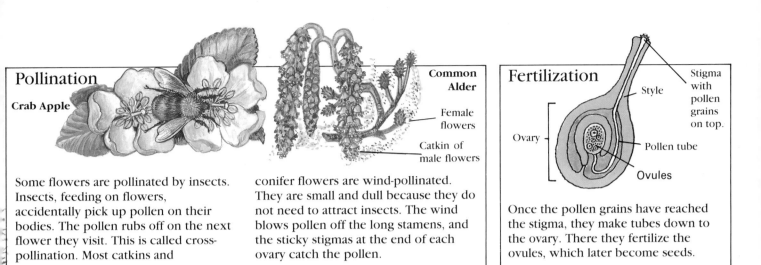

Pollination

Crab Apple

Common Alder

Female flowers

Catkin of male flowers

Some flowers are pollinated by insects. Insects, feeding on flowers, accidentally pick up pollen on their bodies. The pollen rubs off on the next flower they visit. This is called cross-pollination. Most catkins and conifer flowers are wind-pollinated. They are small and dull because they do not need to attract insects. The wind blows pollen off the long stamens, and the sticky stigmas at the end of each ovary catch the pollen.

Fertilization

Stigma with pollen grains on top.

Style

Ovary

Pollen tube

Ovules

Once the pollen grains have reached the stigma, they make tubes down to the ovary. There they fertilize the ovules, which later become seeds.

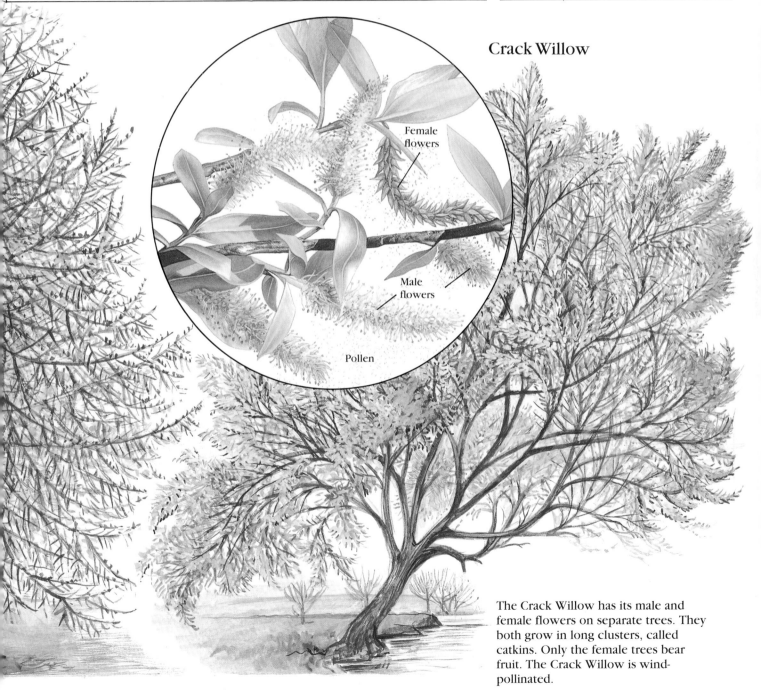

Crack Willow

Female flowers

Male flowers

Pollen

The Crack Willow has its male and female flowers on separate trees. They both grow in long clusters, called catkins. Only the female trees bear fruit. The Crack Willow is wind-pollinated.

Fruits and seeds

Fruits containing seeds grow from fertilized flowers. An apple and the prickly conker case of the Horse Chestnut are both fruits. They look different, but they do the same job, protecting the seeds and helping them to spread to a place where they can grow.

Broadleaved trees have fruits which completely encase their seeds. These fruits can come in many different forms, such as nuts, berries and soft fruits. Conifer seeds are uncovered and not in a fruit that encases them. They are usually held in a scaly cone.

Many fruits and cones are damaged by insects and disease, eaten by birds and animals, or fall off the trees before they can ripen. The seeds inside undamaged healthy fruits ripen in the autumn. They need to get far away from the parent tree, as it will take all the food and light.

Seeds are spread by birds, animals, wind and water. Very few seeds ever get to a place where they can reach full growth. About one in a million acorns becomes an Oak tree.

How a cone ripens

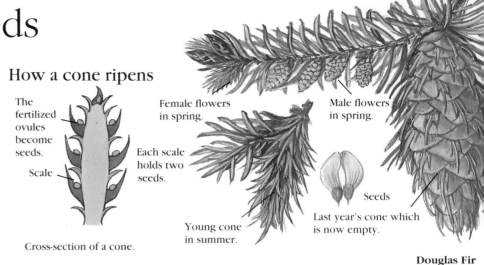

The fertilized ovules become seeds.

Scale

Cross-section of a cone.

Female flowers in spring.

Each scale holds two seeds.

Young cone in summer.

Male flowers in spring.

Seeds

Last year's cone which is now empty.

Douglas Fir

Cones develop from the female flowers. After pollination, the scales harden and close. The stalk often bends, so the cone hangs down. The cone turns from green to brown. When the seeds are ripe and the weather is warm and dry, the scales open. The seeds flutter out on papery wings. Most cones stay on the tree for a year. Others take two years to ripen, and some remain after the seeds have gone.

Fruits of conifers

Most cones have woody scales and vary in size from 1 cm to 35 cm, and can weigh as much as 2 kg. See how many different kinds of cones you can collect.

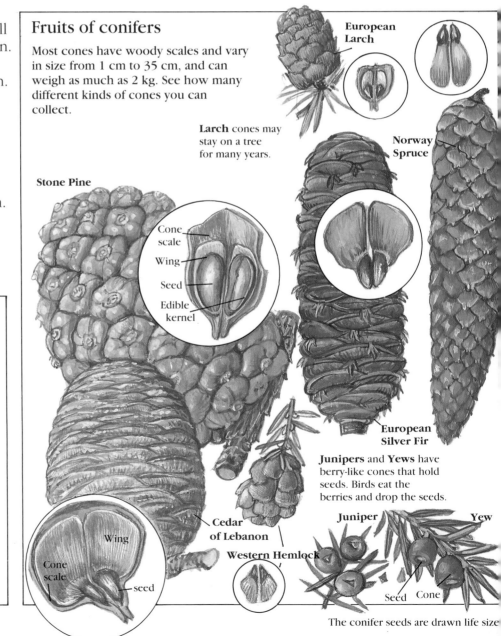

European Larch

Larch cones may stay on a tree for many years.

Stone Pine

Cone scale

Wing

Seed

Edible kernel

Norway Spruce

European Silver Fir

Cedar of Lebanon

Wing

Cone scale

seed

Western Hemlock

Junipers and **Yews** have berry-like cones that hold seeds. Birds eat the berries and drop the seeds.

Juniper

Yew

Seed   Cone

The conifer seeds are drawn life size

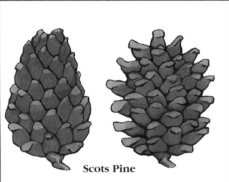

Scots Pine

Cones open in warm, dry weather to release the seeds. If it is wet, the scales close. Find a cone and make it open by placing it near a heater. Then put it in a damp place, and it will close.

How the fruit of a Peach tree ripens

The surrounding ovary becomes the stone which protects the seed.

Flower

The fertilized ovule grows into the seed.

The juicy covering grows from the stem.

Fruit

Ripe fruit of the **Peach** tree.

Ripe fruit of the Peach tree.

The pictures show how the different parts of a flower grow into the different parts of a fruit. The flower is from a Peach tree.

Water from the stem and sunshine make the fleshy part of the fruit swell. As the fruit ripens, it turns golden pink and

softens. The bright colour and sweet smell attract animals or people, who eat thee juicy outer layer and throw away the stone.

Fruits of broadleaved trees

Broadleaved trees produce many different kinds of fruits. Some are nuts with hard outer shells, some are soft fruits, some are pods, some have wings or hairs.

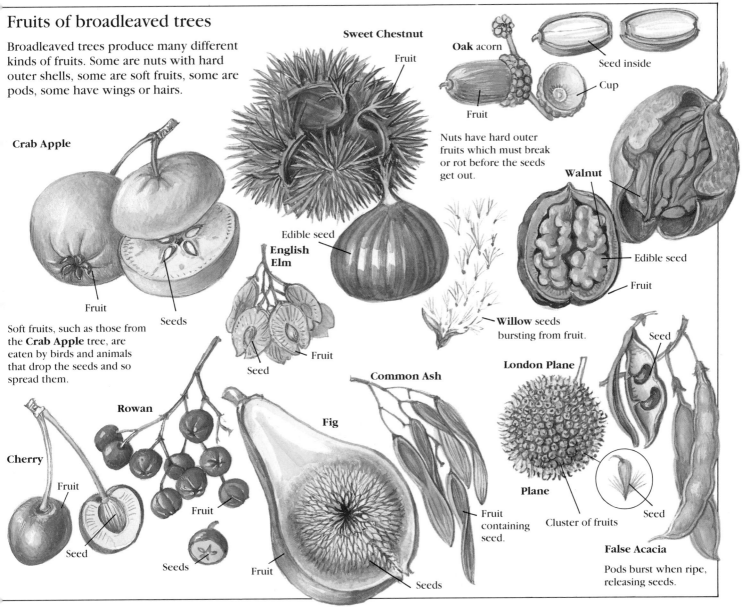

Sweet Chestnut

Fruit

Oak acorn

Seed inside

Cup

Fruit

Nuts have hard outer fruits which must break or rot before the seeds get out.

Walnut

Edible seed

Fruit

Crab Apple

Fruit

Seeds

Soft fruits, such as those from the **Crab Apple** tree, are eaten by birds and animals that drop the seeds and so spread them.

Edible seed

English Elm

Seed

Fruit

Willow seeds bursting from fruit.

London Plane

Seed

Cherry

Fruit

Seed

Rowan

Fruit

Fruit

Seeds

Fig

Fruit

Seeds

Common Ash

Fruit containing seed.

Plane

Cluster of fruits

Seed

False Acacia

Pods burst when ripe, releasing seeds.

The cones and fruits are drawn two thirds life size.

Grow your own tree seedling

Try growing your own tree from a seed. Pick ripe seeds from trees or collect them from the ground if you know that they are fresh. The time a seed takes to sprout varies, but an acorn takes about two months. Some seeds, like those from conifers, may need to lie in the ground for over a year. Once the seedling has sprouted, keep a diary of its growth with drawings or photographs.

What you need

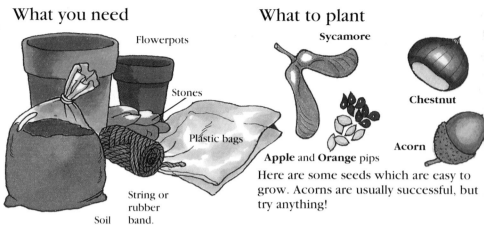

Flowerpots

Stones

Plastic bags

String or rubber band.

Soil

What to plant

Sycamore

Chestnut

Acorn

Apple and **Orange** pips

Here are some seeds which are easy to grow. Acorns are usually successful, but try anything!

1 Soak acorns or other hard nuts in warm water overnight. Peel off the hard outer shells. Do not cut shells from nuts.

2 Put a handful of stones in the bottom of your pot. This is to help the water to drain properly. Place a saucer under the pot.

3 Fill a pot with some soil, or compost, until it is about two thirds full. Water the soil until it is moist, but not soggy.

4 Place one acorn, or other nut, on top of the soil. They need lots of room to grow, so only put one acorn in each pot.

5 Cover the acorn, or other nut, with a layer of soil. This layer should be about as thick as the acorn itself.

Fasten with string or rubber band.

6 Place a plastic bag over the pot. This will keep the seed moist without watering. Put the pot in a sunny place and wait.

The soil should be moist, but not wet.

7 As soon as the seedling appears, remove the plastic bag. Water the seedling once or twice a week.

8 In the summer, put your seedling outside, if you can. In autumn, plant it in the ground. (You can leave it in its pot.)

9 Dig a hole a bit larger than the pot. Gently lift out the seedling and soil from the pot. Plant it in the hole and water it.

Forestry

Trees have been growing on Earth for about 350 million years. Much land was once covered by natural forests, but they have been cut down for timber and cleared. New forests are often planted to replace the trees that have been cut down.

Because conifers grow faster than broadleaved trees and produce straight timber, they are preferred for wood production.

On this page you can read about the story of a Douglas Fir plantation, and what the foresters do to care for the trees.

Seedbeds

The seeds are sown in seedbeds. When the seedlings are 15-20 cm high, they are planted in rows in another bed where they have more room. They are weeded regularly.

Planting out

When the seedlings are about 50 cm high, they are planted out in the forest ground, which has been cleared and ploughed. There are about 2,500 trees per hectare.

Fire towers on hills help to spot fire - the forest's worst enemy. Fires can be started by a carelessly dropped match or an unguarded campfire.

Plantations can be sprayed with weedkillers and fertilizers from the air.

When the trees are felled, they are taken away to sawmills to be cut up.

Every few years the weaker trees are weeded out to give more light and room to the stronger ones. These thinnings are used for poles or are made into paper.

Trees are felled when they are fully grown (about 70 years for conifers and 150 years for Oaks). About one in every ten trees reaches its full growth.

Dead and lower branches are cut off trees. This lessens the risk of fire and stops knots from forming in the wood.

Annual rings

Inside the bark is the wood which is made up of many layers (see page 37). Each year the cambium makes a ring of wood on its inner side and grows outwards. This layer is called an annual ring. The early wood made in spring is pale and has wide tubes (phloem) to carry sap. Late wood, which is formed in summer, is darker and stronger. In wet years, the layers of wood are broad and the annual rings are far apart, but in dry years they are narrow. They are also narrow if the trees are not thinned.

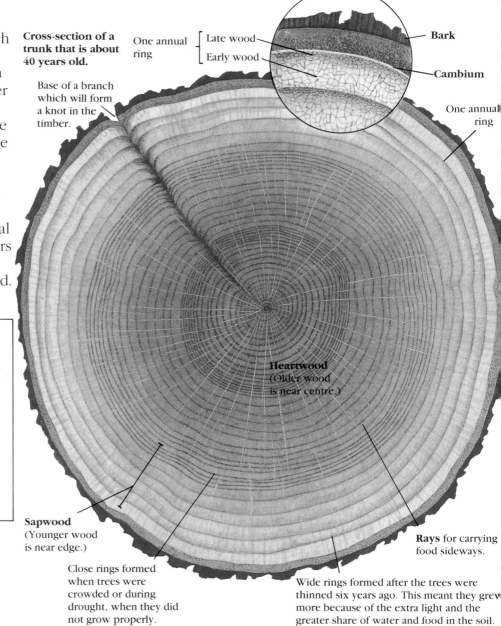

Cross-section of a trunk that is about 40 years old.

Base of a branch which will form a knot in the timber.

One annual ring

Late wood

Early wood

Bark

Cambium

One annual ring

Heartwood (Older wood is near centre.)

Sapwood (Younger wood is near edge.)

Rays for carrying food sideways.

Close rings formed when trees were crowded or during drought, when they did not grow properly.

Wide rings formed after the trees were thinned six years ago. This meant they grew more because of the extra light and the greater share of water and food in the soil.

Palms

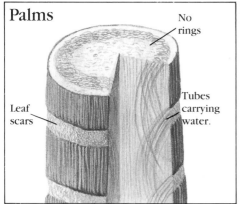

No rings

Leaf scars

Tubes carrying water.

Palm trees do not have annual rings because they have no cambium to grow new wood. Their trunks are like giant stalks which do not grow thicker.

How old is a tree?

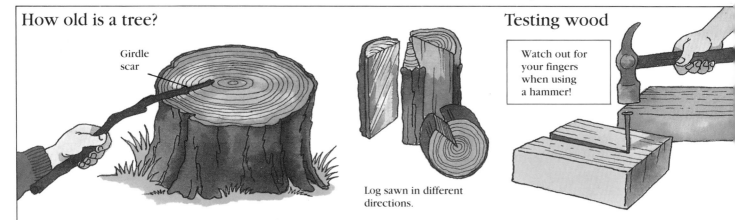

Girdle scar

Log sawn in different directions.

You can find out the age of a tree by counting the annual rings in a cross-section of its trunk, as in this tree stump here. It is easiest to count the dark rings

of late wood. Twigs also have annual layers. Cut off a twig on the slant and count its rings. Then count the girdle scars on the outside. Do they agree?

Testing wood

Watch out for your fingers when using a hammer!

Saw a small log in different ways and look at the patterns the wood makes. Test the strength of different woods by hammering nails into them.

Wood

The wood inside different types of trees varies in colour and pattern, just as the bark varies. Different kinds of wood are suited for certain uses. Wood from conifers, called softwood, is mainly used for building and making paper. Wood from broadleaved trees, called hardwood, is used to make furniture.

At the sawmill, the person operating the saw decides the best way to cut each log. A log can be made into many different sizes of planks, as well as into paper pulp.

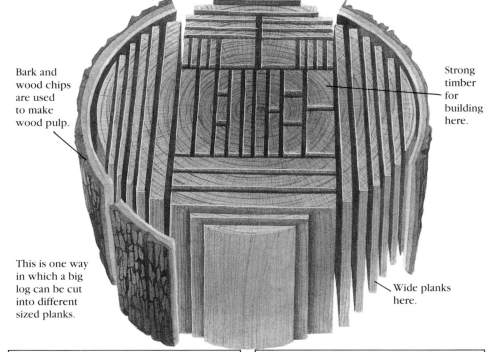

Bark and wood chips are used to make wood pulp.

Strong timber for building here.

This is one way in which a big log can be cut into different sized planks.

Wide planks here.

Grain

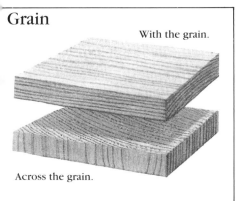

With the grain.

Across the grain.

When a plank is cut from a log, the annual rings make vertical lines which may be wavy or straight. This pattern is called the grain. Wood cut with the grain is stronger than wood cut across the grain..

Knots

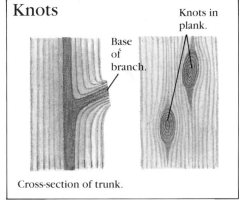

Knots in plank.

Base of branch.

Cross-section of trunk.

In a plank you may notice dark spots, called knots. This is where the base of a branch was buried in the trunk of the tree. This distorts and colours the grain, and so leaves a knot.

Seasoning

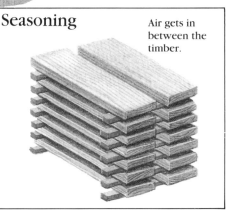

Air gets in between the timber.

Fresh wood contains water which is why green logs spit in the fire. As wood dries, it shrinks and often cracks or warps. Planks must be dried out, or seasoned, before they can be used.

Processed wood

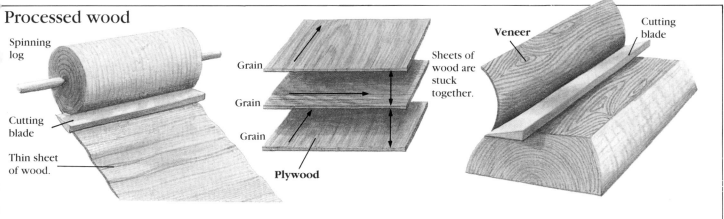

Spinning log

Cutting blade

Thin sheet of wood.

Grain

Grain

Grain

Plywood

Sheets of wood are stuck together.

Veneer

Cutting blade

Much of the wood that you see around you has been "processed". Plywood is thin layers of wood which are glued together with the grain lying in different directions. It is stronger than ordinary wood and does not warp. The thin sheet of wood is peeled off the log like a Swiss roll. Veneer is a thin sheet of wood with a beautiful grain which is used on the surface of plain furniture. Chipboard (not shown) is made of small chips and shavings mixed with glue.

53

Pests and fungi

Trees are attacked by insects and diseases caused by fungi. Insects use trees for food and shelter, and as places to breed. They can cause serious damage to trees, but they rarely kill them.

Fungi are a group of plants which do not flower. Mushrooms are fungi. Because fungi cannot make their own food, they may feed off plants and animals, and sometimes kill them. Fungi spread by releasing microscopic spores, like seeds, into the tree. These spores can spread and rot the tree.

Larva

Nut Weevils lay their eggs inside nuts, where the larvae grow.

Adult **Nut Weevil**

Leaves and shoots

Spangle galls

Cherry gall

Pine Looper

Gall Wasp

Kidney galls

Oak apple galls

Pine Sawfly

Green Tortrix

The **Tent Caterpillar** lives in a "tent", which it spins among the branches.

Many moth and butterfly caterpillars and other larvae eat leaves. Often each species only feeds on a certain type of tree.

Leaf Roller

Leaf Miner

Leaf Miners eat tunnels through leaves. **Leaf Rollers** fold leaves over themselves for protection.

Aphid

Some insects lay their eggs in leaves or shoots. The tree forms swellings, called galls, around the eggs. The larvae feed inside the galls.

"Pineapple" gall

An **Aphid** made this "pineapple" gall by piercing a shoot to suck out the sap.

Bark and wood

Conifer Heart Rot is caused by this bracket fungus. It attacks conifers and rots the inside of trees until they die.

White Pine Blister Rust is a fungus which causes swellings on pine trunks and branches.

Look for **Scale** insects on bark. If you pull one off, you may see the grub which sucks sap from the tree.

Elm Bark Beetles make tunnels under Elm bark. They spread the fungus which causes Dutch Elm Disease.

Honey Fungus attacks the roots of many trees. In autumn, their toadstools appear at the base of infected trees.

The **Pine Weevil** strips the bark off newly planted conifers.

Roots

Gall Wasp

Some **Gall Wasps** lay their eggs on Oak roots. Galls with the larvae inside swell up on the roots.

Some moth caterpillars also eat roots while living underground.

The **Cockchafer Beetle** larva lives in the ground feeding on the roots of young trees.

54

Keeping an Oak apple gall

Netting top tied on with string.

Release **Wasp** when it emerges.

Oak Apple

In summer, collect Oak apples and other galls which do not have holes in them. Keep them in a jar with netting on top. The wasps living inside the galls should emerge in a month.

Making spore prints

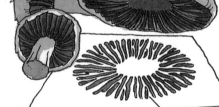

Mushrooms or toadstools

Cap

Spore print

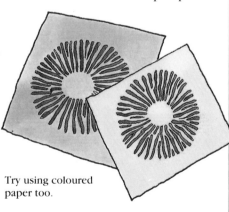

Try using coloured paper too.

Make spore prints from mushrooms. Cut off the stalk and place the cap on some paper. Leave it overnight. It will release its spores on the paper, leaving a print. Always wash your hands after handling a fungus.

Injuries

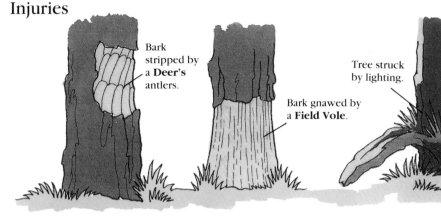

Bark stripped by a **Deer's** antlers.

Bark gnawed by a **Field Vole**.

Tree struck by lighting.

Sometimes trees are damaged by animals. Deer strip the bark off trees when they scrape the "velvet" off their antlers. Squirrels, voles and rabbits eat young bark, which can kill young saplings. If lightning strikes a tree, the trunk often cracks. This happens because the sap gets so hot that it becomes steam. It expands and then explodes, shattering the tree.

How a tree heals itself

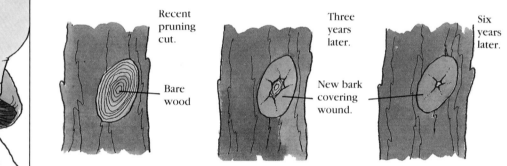

Recent pruning cut.

Bare wood

Three years later.

New bark covering wound.

Six years later.

If a branch is pruned off a tree properly, the wound usually heals. A new rim of bark grows from the cambium around the cut. This finished seal will keep out fungi and diseases. It takes years for a wound to heal. But if a wound completely surrounds the trunk, the tree will die because its food supply is cut off. This can happen when animals strip off the bark.

How trees die

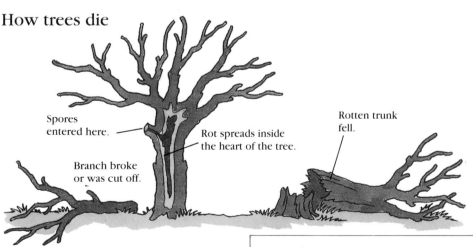

Spores entered here.

Branch broke or was cut off.

Rot spreads inside the heart of the tree.

Rotten trunk fell.

Fungus kills many trees. Spores in the air enter an opening and spread through the tree. The heartwood rots until the tree dies and falls down.

Remember! Never carve your initials or anything else on a tree. It looks ugly and can leave an opening for fungi to enter.

Woodland life

The forest is home to many plants and animals. Trees protect wildlife from bad weather, wind and too much sun. Fallen leaves and twigs make a rich soil called humus. This helps plants to grow. The wildlife in broadleaved and coniferous forests is not the same, although it may overlap.

Trees change carbon dioxide into oxygen. Chopping down trees leaves too much carbon dioxide in the atmosphere which is bad for our planet, making it warmer. This is called the "greenhouse" effect.

A coniferous forest

A coniferous forest is dark and dense. Few plants grow on the ground because of the thick layer of needles and the lack of light. Here are some animals and plants you might see in a coniferous forest.

Pine Marten

Squirrel's drey

Long-eared Owl's nest

Great Spotted Woodpecker

Long-eared Owl

Red Deer

Crossbill

Bracken

Black Grouse

Norway spruce cones

Fox

Wood Ant-hill

Broad Buckler Fern

Timberman

Goldcrest

Fly Agaric

Treecreeper

Red Squirrel

Lichen

Black Slug

56

A broadleaved forest

A broadleaved forest is more light and open and so attracts many more plants and animals. There are many flowers in spring before the trees' leaves have blocked out the light. As you can see, an Oak wood supports many different kinds of wildlife.

Tree roots help to hold the soil firm. If forests are cut down and the land cleared, the soil can become very loose and dry. This is called erosion.

Mistletoe

Nuthatch

Green Woodpecker

Rook in nest

Tawny Owl

Blue Tit

Long-eared Bat in tree

Poor Man's Beefsteak

Oak

Wood Anemone

Roe Deer

Badger

Bluebells

Rabbit

Pheasant

Ivy

Common Shrew

Hedgehog

Primrose

Moss

Common Toad

Earthworm

Greater Stag Beetle

Speckled Wood Butterfly

57

Making a tree survey

You will gather many interesting facts about trees and the wildlife they shelter by doing a tree survey. Start with a small area and choose one that has many trees of different types. A piece of countryside, a park, garden or street will all do.

With a friend, make a rough map of your area and add any landmarks, such as roads or buildings. Try to work out a scale for your map - 2 cm for every 50 paces is a good one. Plot each tree on your map and be careful not to miss any.

What to take

Notebook

Tree field guide

Tape measure

Pencils

String

Identifying a tree

Try to identify the trees using this book or another guide. Remember that there are many clues to help you identify them. One type of clue, such as a leaf, is not enough.

Making a map

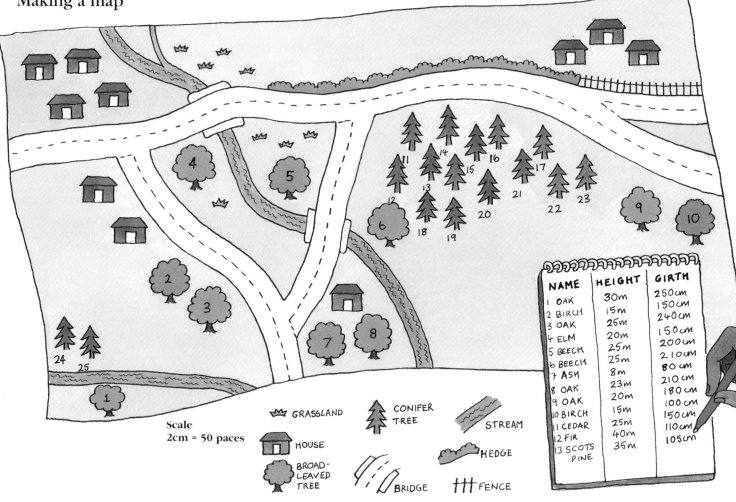

Scale
2cm = 50 paces

GRASSLAND

HOUSE

BROAD-LEAVED TREE

CONIFER TREE

BRIDGE

STREAM

HEDGE

FENCE

NAME	HEIGHT	GIRTH
1 OAK	30m	250cm
2 BIRCH	15m	150cm
3 OAK	25m	240cm
4 ELM	20m	150cm
5 BEECH	25m	200cm
6 BEECH	25m	210cm
7 ASH	8m	80cm
8 OAK	23m	210cm
9 OAK	20m	180cm
10 BIRCH	15m	100cm
11 CEDAR	25m	150cm
12 FIR	40m	110cm
13 SCOTS PINE	35m	105cm

After you have identified and measured the trees (as shown on these pages), make a neater and more detailed copy of your map. Show the scale of your map. Then make a key of the symbols you used, like the one above.

Write down the findings of your survey. Give the name, height and girth of each tree. Repeat the survey later to see if there are any new trees, or if anything else has changed. If you enjoyed making the survey, you can write to the Tree Council * to find out how to do a more complicated one.

 *Tree Council, 35 Belgrave Square, London Sw1 8QB

Measuring a tree

Mark stick here where your thumb lined up with your friend's feet.

The friend here is 1.5 m tall.

The tree here is four times the height of your friend. 4 x 1.5 m = 6 m. This is the height of the tree.

Ask a friend to stand by a tree. From a short distance, hold up a stick at arm's length. Line up the stick's tip with the top of your friend's head. Then move your thumb up the stick until it lines up with your friend's feet. Mark the stick where your thumb is.

From the same spot, hold out the stick again. How many times does the piece of stick above the mark go into the height of the tree. (Look carefully at the pictures here to see how this is done.) Now multiply the answer by your friend's height (1.5 m here).

Measure the girth of a tree at chest height. Ask your friend to hold one end of some string while you hold the other. Walk right around the tree until you meet your friend. Now measure the length of string.

Studying a tree

Make a careful study of one tree all through the year. Choose a tree which you can get to easily and often. Make a notebook in which you keep a record of when it comes into leaf, when it flowers and fruits, and when it drops its leaves. Include sketches or photos of the tree at these different times and keep specimens from it.

Squirrel's drey

Insects on the bark.

Nest

Do not touch birds' nests or go too near to them.

White sheet to catch insects.

Study the animals that live in or near your tree. Look for birds' nests and squirrels' dreys in the tree top. Look on the trunk for insects and on the ground for other traces of animals, such as owl pellets, and nuts or cones which have been eaten by animals. To examine the insects in the tree, beat a branch gently with a stick. With a white sheet, catch the insects that fall out.

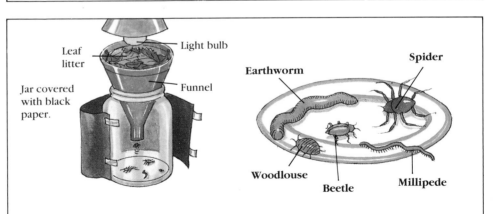

Leaf litter

Light bulb

Jar covered with black paper.

Funnel

Earthworm

Spider

Woodlouse

Beetle

Millipede

Leaf litter is made up of dead and rotting leaves and contains many small animals. To study these animals, take a large funnel (or make one out of tin foil), and place it in a jar. Cover the jar with black paper. Fill the funnel with damp leaf litter. Place a lamp about 10 cm above the leaves and switch it on. Wait a few hours. The heat and light from the lamp will drive the animals into the dark jar. Then you can take them out and study them.

Common trees you can spot

Conifers

Lawson Cypress 25 m. Narrow shape. Drooping top shoot. Small, round cones. Common as a hedge.

Cones

Western Red Cedar 30 m. Branches curve upwards. Tiny, flower-like cones. Hedges.

Seed

Cone

Yew 15 m. Dark green. Trunk gnarled. Bark reddish. Leaves and red-berried fruits poisonous.

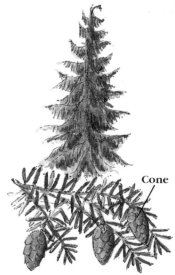

Cone

Western Hemlock 35 m. Branches and top shoot droop. Small cones. Needles various lengths.

Cone

Norway Spruce 30 m. Christmas tree. Long, hanging cones. Parks, gardens, plantations.

Cone

Douglas Fir 40 m. Hanging, shaggy cones. Deep-ridged bark. Important timber tree.

Cone

European Silver Fir 40 m. Large, upright cones at top of tree. Parklands.

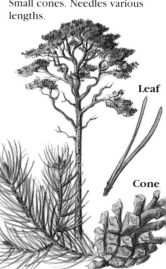

Leaf

Cone

Scots Pine 35 m. Uneven crown. Bare trunk. Flaking bark. Common wild and planted.

Cone

Corsican Pine 36 m. Shape rounder and fuller than Scots Pine. Long, dark green needles. Dark brown bark.

Blue Atlas Cedar 25 m. Broad shape. Barrel-shaped, upright cones. Blue-green needles. Parks.

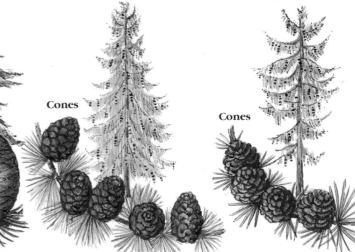

Cones

European Larch 38 m. Upright cones egg-shaped. Soft, light-green needles fall off in winter.

Cones

Japanese Larch 35 m. Upright, rosette-like cones. Orange twigs. Blue-green needles fall in winter.

Broadleaved trees

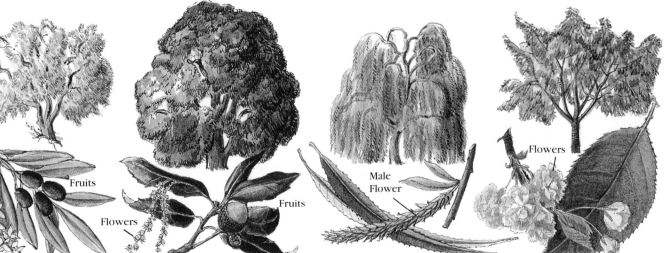

Olive 10 m. Evergreen. Twisted grey trunk. Black edible fruits. Southern Europe.

Holm Oak 20 m. Evergreen. Shiny leaves resemble Holly. Grey bark. Parks and gardens.

Weeping Willow 20 m. Drooping shape. Near water and in gardens.

Japanese Cherry 9 m. Flowers April-May. Many varieties. Gardens and along streets.

Wild Cherry or **Gean** 15 m. Red-brown bark peels in ribbons. Flowers April-May. Fruits sour. Woods, thickets.

Almond 8 m. Flowers March-April before leaves. Edible nut inside green fruit. Gardens.

Holly 10 m. Evergreen. Leaves often variegated. Berries posionous. Often shrub-like.

Sweet Chestnut 35 m. Spiral-ridged bark. Two edible nuts in prickly green case. Wide-spreading branches.

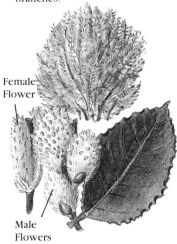

Crab Apple 10 m. Small tree. Flowers May. Fruits edible but sour. Wild in hedges and thickets.

Common Pear 15 m. Straight trunk. Flowers April-May. Edible fruits. Hedgerows and gardens.

Orange 9 m. Evergreen. Many varieties. Fragrant flowers in winter. Fruits edible. Southern Europe.

Goat or **Pussy Willow** 7 m. Catkins March-April. Separate male and female trees. Hedges and damp woodlands.

The trees are arranged by leaf shape. The height given is of a large full-grown tree.

More broadleaved trees

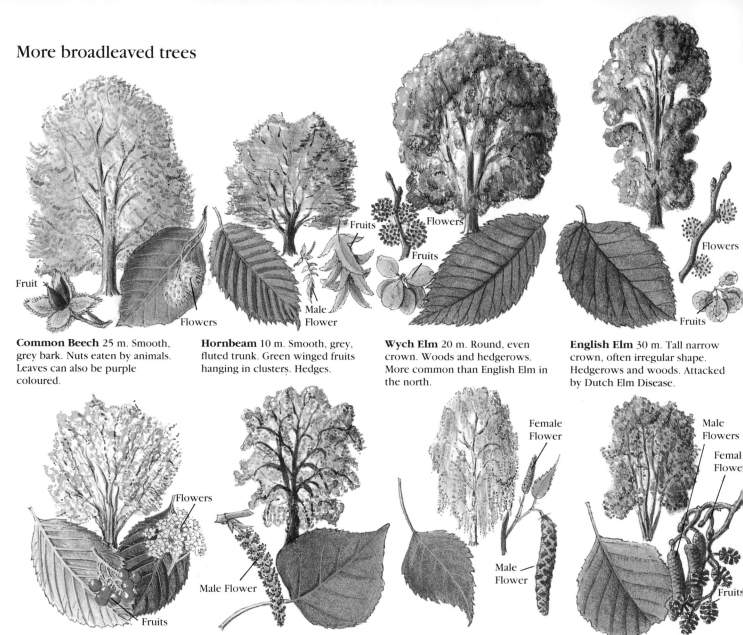

Common Beech 25 m. Smooth, grey bark. Nuts eaten by animals. Leaves can also be purple coloured.

Hornbeam 10 m. Smooth, grey, fluted trunk. Green winged fruits hanging in clusters. Hedges.

Wych Elm 20 m. Round, even crown. Woods and hedgerows. More common than English Elm in the north.

English Elm 30 m. Tall narrow crown, often irregular shape. Hedgerows and woods. Attacked by Dutch Elm Disease.

Whitebeam 8 m. Leaves white-felted underneath. Flowers May-June. Sour red berries. Grows wild.

Black Poplar 25 m. Dark trunk often with bumps. Common in city parks.

Silver Birch 15 m. White bark peels in ribbons. "Lamb's tail" catkins in April. Wild on heaths and mountains. Planted in gardens.

Common Alder 12 m. Cone-like fruits which stay on in winter. Catkins in early spring. Near water and damp woodlands.

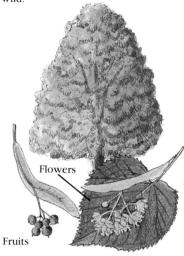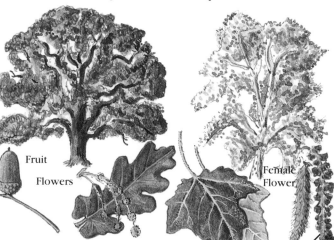

Common Lime 25 m. Heart-shaped leaves. Fragrant flowers attract bees in June. Parks and gardens.

Turkey Oak 25 m. Whiskers on buds and at base of leaves. Acorn cups mossy. Bark ridged.

English or **Pedunculate Oak** 23 m. Wide-spreading branches. Long-stalked acorns. Common alone and in woods.

White Poplar 20 m. Leaves covered with white down underneath. Bark whitish-grey with diamond marks.

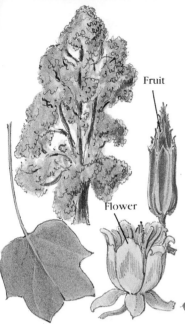

Tulip Tree 20 m. Tulip-like flowers, June-July. Upright brown fruits. Parks, gardens.

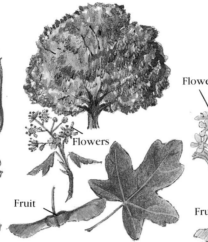

Field Maple 10 m. Rounded crown. Narrow-ridged bark. Winged seeds almost form straight line. Hedges and woods.

Norway Maple 15 m. Seeds form wide angle. Autumn leaves colourful. Parks, streets.

Sycamore 20 m. Seeds form close angle. Smooth bark flakes off in plates. Parks, streets.

London Plane 30 m. Bark flakes off leaving white patches. Spiky fruits stay on in winter. City streets.

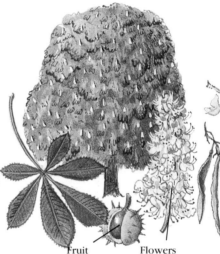

Fig 6 m. Flower inside a pear-shaped receptacle which becomes the fruit. Gardens.

Horse Chestnut 25 m. Compound leaves. Upright flowers, May. Prickly fruits with conkers inside.

Laburnum or **Golden Rain** 7 m. Compound leaves. Flowers May-June. Seeds poisonous. Gardens.

False Acacia or **Locust Tree** 20 m. Compound leaves. Ridged twigs spiny. Hanging flowers, in June. Gardens, parks.

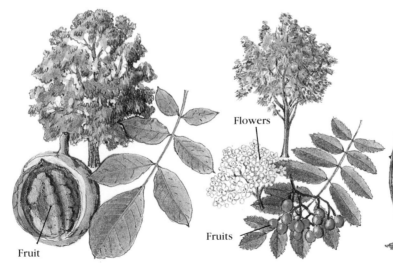

Walnut 15 m. Compound leaves. Deep-ridged bark. Hollow twigs. Edible nuts inside thick green fruits.

Rowan or **Mountain Ash** 7 m. Compound leaves. Flowers May. Sour orange berries, September. Wild on mountains.

Common Ash 25 m. Compound leaves open late. Key-shaped fruits stay on in winter. Common woods, parks.

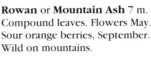

Trees in winter

Norway spruce

Monkey Puzzle (Chile Pine)

Corsican pine

Maidenhair Tree (Ginkgo)

Cedar of Lebanon

Italian Cypress

Strawberry Tree

Big Tree (Wellingtonia)

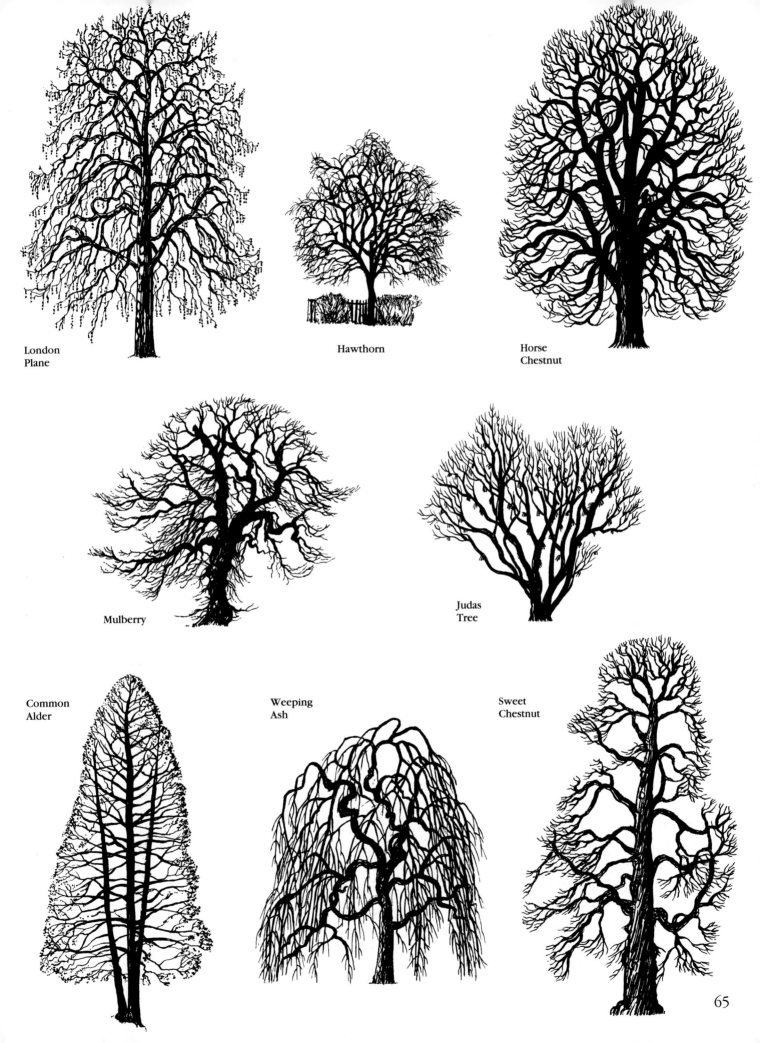

London
Plane

Hawthorn

Horse
Chestnut

Mulberry

Judas
Tree

Common
Alder

Weeping
Ash

Sweet
Chestnut

65

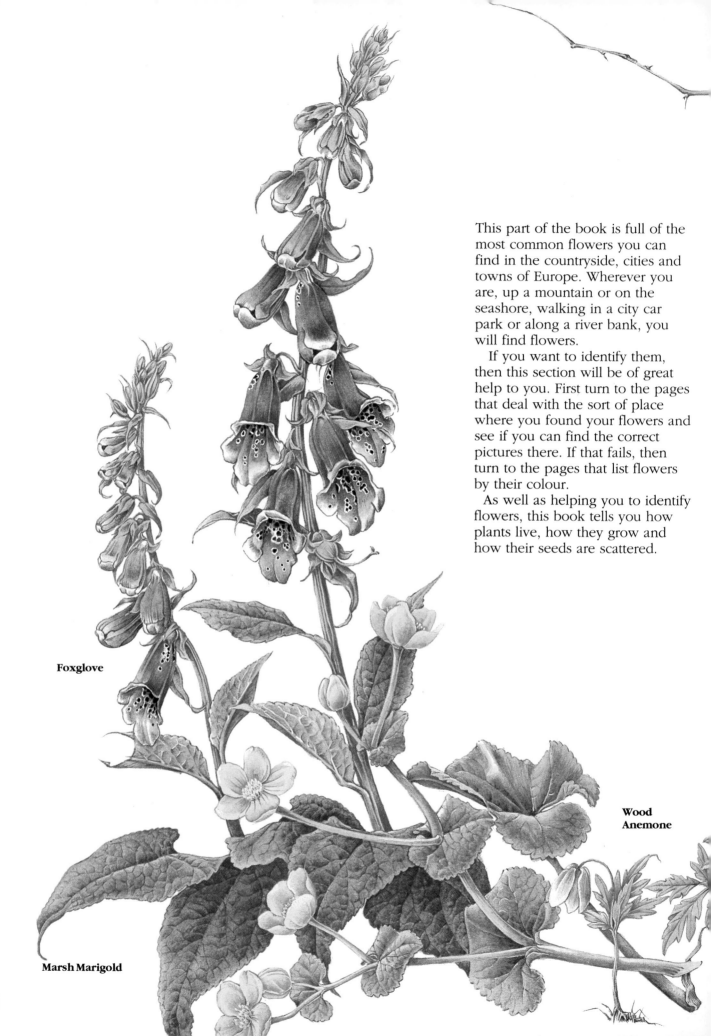

This part of the book is full of the most common flowers you can find in the countryside, cities and towns of Europe. Wherever you are, up a mountain or on the seashore, walking in a city car park or along a river bank, you will find flowers.

If you want to identify them, then this section will be of great help to you. First turn to the pages that deal with the sort of place where you found your flowers and see if you can find the correct pictures there. If that fails, then turn to the pages that list flowers by their colour.

As well as helping you to identify flowers, this book tells you how plants live, how they grow and how their seeds are scattered.

Foxglove

Wood Anemone

Marsh Marigold

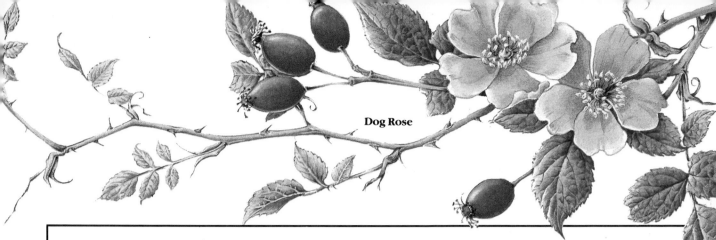

Dog Rose

WILD FLOWERS

Contents

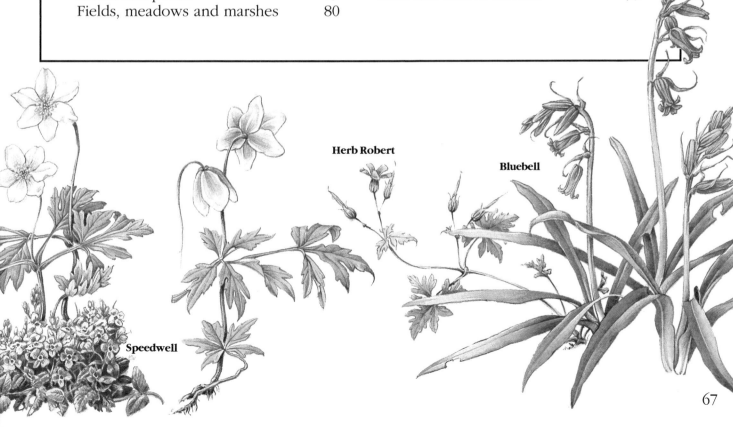

Herb Robert

Bluebell

Speedwell

Looking for wild flowers

When you go looking for wild flowers, take a notebook with you and two pencils for making notes and quick sketches. A tape measure, magnifying glass and outdoor thermometer are useful too. Record all you can about a flower, such as its height, colour and where it is growing. Use the magnifying glass to study the small parts.

Never dig up flowers and only pick them if you are sure they are common and there are lots of the same kind growing together. Take sheets of blotting paper to press them.

JULY 12th 1991
STOUR MEADOWS 20°C

flowers are yellow

flower heads are 20mm across

flowers are flat on top

flowers look like a daisy

Plant has hairs

leaves are oval and pointed at ends

Plant is 40cm high

leaves have wavy edges

This is what the inside of a buttercup looks like. Other flowers may look different. Try to draw what you see inside the flower you have found.

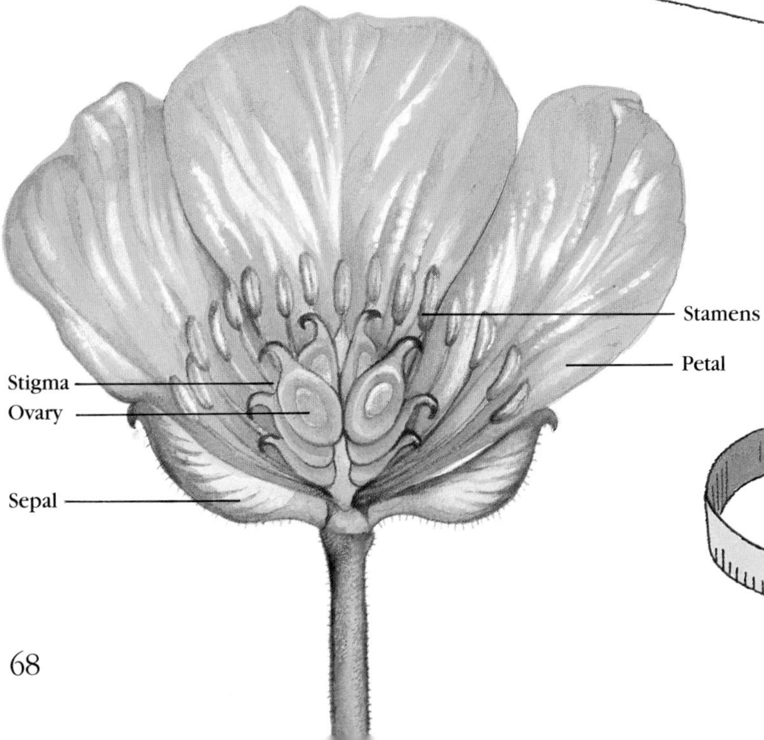

Stamens

Petal

Stigma

Ovary

Sepal

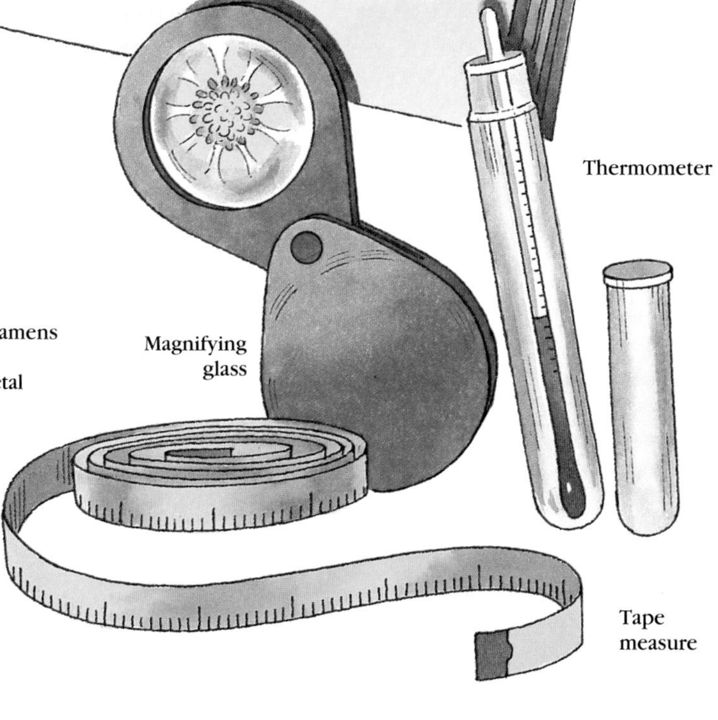

Magnifying glass

Thermometer

Tape measure

Rare flowers

The three flowers shown on the right are very rare indeed. If you think you may have found a rare flower, do not pick it. If you do, the flower will become even more rare and it may disappear completely from the spot where you found it.

Instead, make a careful drawing of the flower and record in your notebook exactly where you found it. Show these to an adult who knows about rare flowers. If it is rare, you can report it to a conservation or nature club.

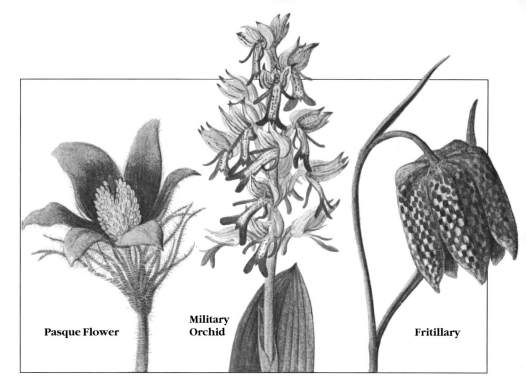

Pasque Flower

Military Orchid

Fritillary

How to make a flower map

The easiest way to make a map is to draw it as you walk along a route you know well. Draw lines for a road or path and make them turn in the same way you do.

Put in symbols for bridges, buildings and other special places. Wherever you find wild flowers, mark the place with a star. Use different colour stars for different types of flowers. Draw the symbols on the bottom of your map and write down next to them what they mean, so that everyone can understand them.

If you like, you can use a scale to show distance. Then anyone looking at it can understand how far apart everything is.

You can choose any scale you want. This map has a scale of 2 cm for every 50 paces.

SYMBOLS FOR YOUR MAP

★ FLOWERS
🌳 WOODS
〜 STREAM
⊻ GRASSLAND
▲ HILLS
↓ MARSHES, WATER
▤ BRIDGE
🏠 HOUSES

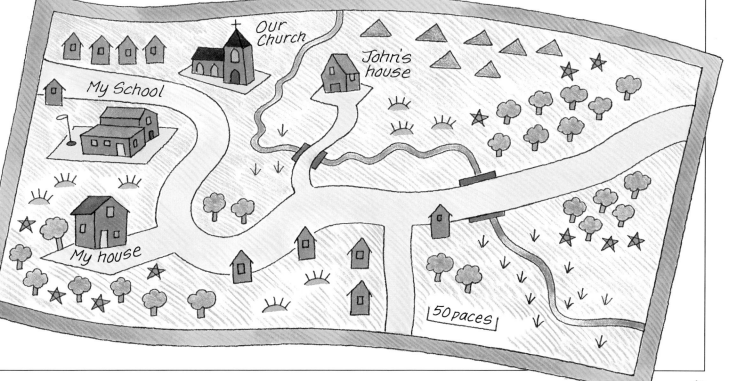

How plants live

The Rosebay Willowherb and the Field Buttercup have flowers with petals and sepals. They also have leaves, stems and roots. Most other plants have the same parts, but they can be different shapes and sizes.

Each part of a plant does one special thing that helps the plant to live. Leaves make food for a plant. During the day, they take in a gas from the air called carbon dioxide. This gas, the green colouring in the leaves, water and sunlight are used by the leaves to make food.

Leaves breathe out gases and water and take in gases from the air through tiny holes, so small you cannot see them with a magnifying glass.

Rosebay Willowherb

The **flower** is a very important part of the plant. It is here that the seeds grow.

The **sepals** protect the flower when it is in bud. When the flower is open, they lie underneath the petals. All the sepals together are called the calyx.

The **petals** may be brightly coloured or scented to attract insects. Some flowers need insects to carry pollen to other flowers for pollination (see pages 72 and 74), so the brighter the colours, the more insects the flower will attract.

Field Buttercup

The **leaves** make food and "breathe" for the plant. They also get rid of any water that the plant does not need. Because leaves need light to make food, the whole plant grows towards light. Some plants close their leaves at night.

The **stem** carries water from the roots to the leaves, and carries food made in the leaves to the rest of the plant. It also holds the leaves up to the light.

The **roots** hold the plant firmly in the ground and draw up water from the soil that the plant needs.

How to identify flowers

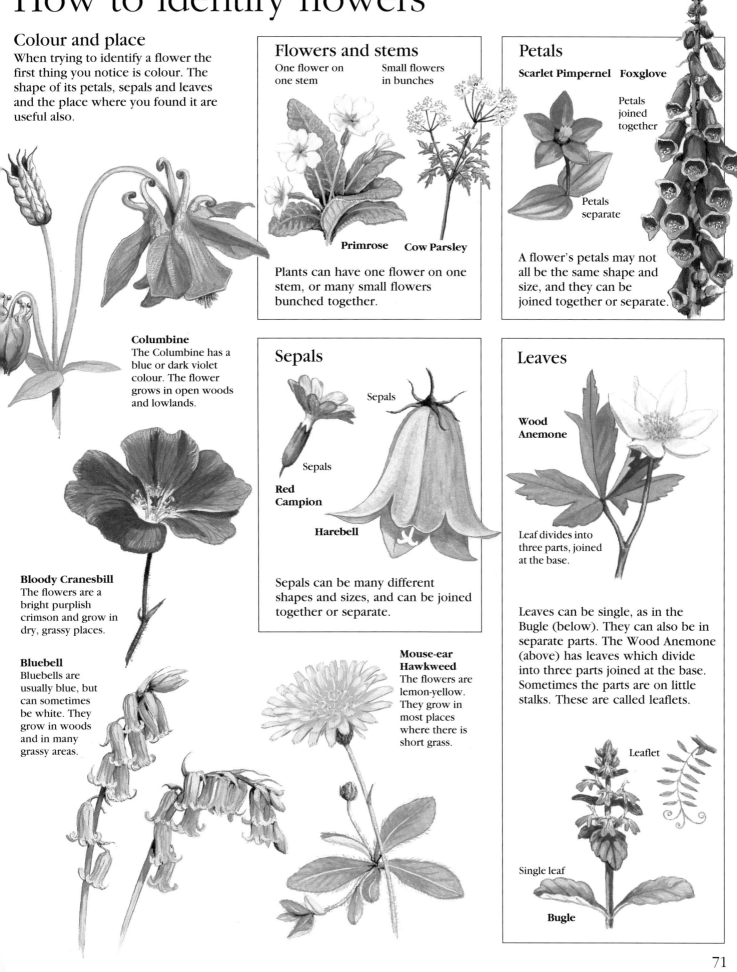

Colour and place

When trying to identify a flower the first thing you notice is colour. The shape of its petals, sepals and leaves and the place where you found it are useful also.

Columbine
The Columbine has a blue or dark violet colour. The flower grows in open woods and lowlands.

Bloody Cranesbill
The flowers are a bright purplish crimson and grow in dry, grassy places.

Bluebell
Bluebells are usually blue, but can sometimes be white. They grow in woods and in many grassy areas.

Flowers and stems

One flower on one stem

Small flowers in bunches

Primrose   **Cow Parsley**

Plants can have one flower on one stem, or many small flowers bunched together.

Petals

Scarlet Pimpernel   **Foxglove**

Petals joined together

Petals separate

A flower's petals may not all be the same shape and size, and they can be joined together or separate.

Sepals

Sepals

Sepals

Red Campion

Harebell

Sepals can be many different shapes and sizes, and can be joined together or separate.

Mouse-ear Hawkweed
The flowers are lemon-yellow. They grow in most places where there is short grass.

Leaves

Wood Anemone

Leaf divides into three parts, joined at the base.

Leaves can be single, as in the Bugle (below). They can also be in separate parts. The Wood Anemone (above) has leaves which divide into three parts joined at the base. Sometimes the parts are on little stalks. These are called leaflets.

Leaflet

Single leaf

Bugle

71

How flowers grow

Almost every plant has a male part, called the stamen, and a female part, called the pistil. The Common Poppy has a group of stamens in the centre of the flower which grow around the pistil (see picture 3).

These pages tell you how the stamens and the pistil in a poppy work together to make seeds and how insects, such as bees, play a very important part by carrying pollen from flower to flower. These seeds will leave the plant and become new plants. Not all plants make seeds in this way, but many do.

1

In the spring, the new plant grows from a seed buried in the ground. Later, many buds will develop on the plant.

Bud

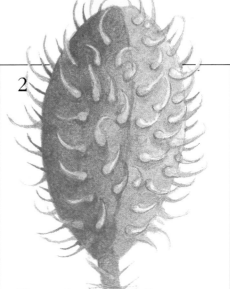

2

The sepals protect the flower when it is inside the bud. As the flower grows, the sepals begin to open.

6 When a bee visits another poppy some of this pollen may fall off onto the other flower's stigma. This is called pollination.

When the pollen grains land on top of the stigma, very thin tubes begin to grow down towards the ovary.

Stamens

Stigma
Pistil
Ovary

The **pistil** has two parts, the **stigma** and the **ovary**. The stigma is the top part. The ovary is the bottom part and holds "eggs", called ovules.

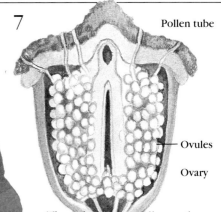

7

Pollen tube

Ovules

Ovary

The tubes eventually reach the ovules in the ovary. The contents of each pollen grain empty into an ovule. This is called fertilization.

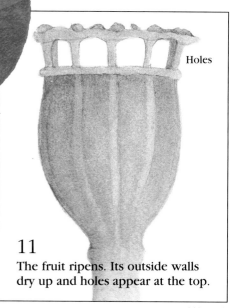

Holes

11

The fruit ripens. Its outside walls dry up and holes appear at the top.

3
In the summer, the petals open. You can see the stamens (the male parts) and the pistil (the female parts).

Pistil

Stamens

4
Pollen

Anther

The small sacs at the end of the stamens, called anthers, open. The powder they hold, called pollen, escapes.

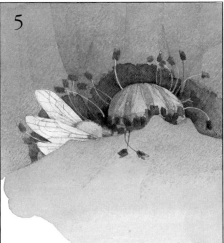

5
When a bee visits a poppy to feed, pollen from the stamens sticks to its hairy body or onto its legs.

8
Once fertilization has taken place, the pollen on the stamens falls off and the stamens and petals wilt.

Pollen

9
Pistil

Petals

Stamens

The poppy does not need the stamens or the petals any more and they fall off. But the pistil is still needed. It remains strong.

10

Fruit

Inside the pistil, the fertilized ovules are growing to form seeds. They are attached to the inside walls of the ovary. At this stage the ovary is called fruit.

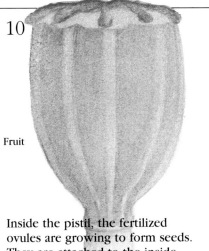

12

Wind

Holes at top of fruit.

Seeds

The seeds break away from the walls inside the fruit. They fall out through holes near the top when the poppy is blown by the wind.

13 The seeds which fall out of the fruit onto the soil in the autumn may grow into new plants the next spring.

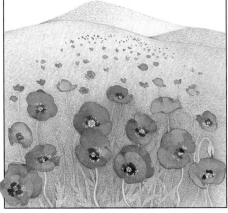

How pollen is spread

In most plants, pollen must travel to another plant of the same sort to make seeds in an ovary. The pollen from a Common Poppy plant can only make seeds in another Common Poppy plant, not the one it came from (see pages 72-73). This is called cross-pollination.

In a few plants, such as the Red Helleborine on this page, pollen can make seeds grow in an ovary from the same flower. This is called self-pollination. Pollen can never make seeds grow in another sort of plant. Pollen from a rose cannot pollinate a daisy.

Insects feed on the nectar inside flowers and they can carry pollen from plant to plant when it sticks to their bodies. The colour of petals or scent can attract insects into the flowers. Some flowers have spots or lines on their petals called nectar guides. The insects follow these guides to find nectar.

The wind carries pollen too and in the summer the air is full of it. It can give people hayfever and make them sneeze.

By insects

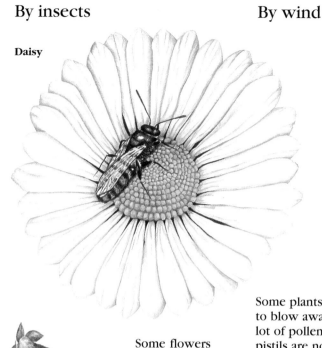

Daisy

Foxglove

Some flowers make the shape of a platform with their petals for insects to land on easily.

Bees crawl inside some flowers to gather nectar.

By wind

Dog's Mercury

Some plants make it easy for the wind to blow away the pollen. They have a lot of pollen, and the stamens and pistils are not covered.

By itself

Red Helleborine

Some flowers, like the Red Helleborine, can pollinate themselves.

What plants need

Plants need to grow, spread their pollen, and make sure their seeds are scattered far away. To do all these things, they often depend on the weather, the soil and other living creatures - even people.

Some plants need insects to carry pollen.

Plants need the right amount of water and mineral salts in the soil to help them grow.

Plants need certain temperatures, whether they grow in cool or hot places. Most European flowers bloom when it is warm.

Plants need light to make food for themselves and to grow.

How seeds are scattered

Once the seeds have grown in the ovaries, it is important that they are scattered. Then they can begin to grow into another plant. Plants need light to grow, so it is best if they fall away from the parent plant, which might overshadow them and block out the light.

Seeds can be scattered by the wind, by animals and by water. Some plants scatter their seeds by themselves.

By animals

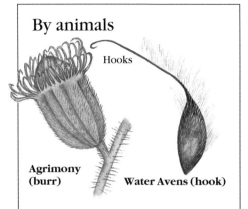

Hooks

Agrimony (burr)

Water Avens (hook)

Some seeds have burrs or hooks that stick to animal fur. The seeds eventually drop off the animal and in this way may be carried far from the parent plant.

By wind

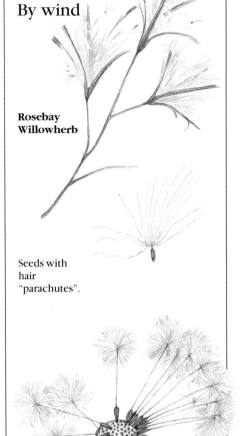

Rosebay Willowherb

Seeds with hair "parachutes".

Dandelion ("clock")

Some seeds can float on the wind. Dandelion seeds are inside very small fruits, which have hairs that behave like parachutes.

By water

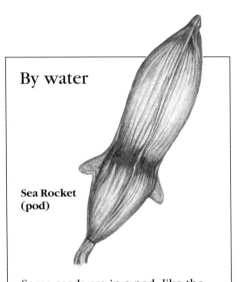

Sea Rocket (pod)

Some seeds are in a pod, like the Sea Rocket pod, that floats in the water until it opens, releasing the seeds.

By explosion

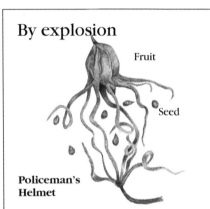

Fruit

Seed

Policeman's Helmet

Some plants have their seeds in a fruit that pops open. The seeds then shoot out, and travel away from the parent plant. The fruits of the Policeman's Helmet do this.

Animals carry seeds and nuts and drop them away from the parent plant.

Some plants need water to carry seeds away from the parent plant.

Birds may fly far from where they eat fruits. The seeds pass through their bodies and fall on the ground.

People often spread seeds without knowing. They get seeds in the soles of their shoes.

Flower record book

You could keep everything you discover about wild flowers in a record book. The best sort of book is a loose-leaf binder, which lets you add pages whenever you wish. This is the perfect place to copy out notes from flower hunting expeditions and keep drawings, maps you have made and photographs.

Everything to do with wild flowers belongs in your book. Record your experiments too. Draw and write about every step of an experiment as it happens.

A flower record book will be a permanent reminder of all the interesting bits of information you discover about the flowers you find.

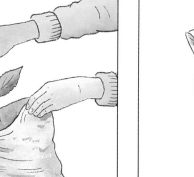

Common Mallow
Found in a grassy field
on July 25th

Stick pressed flowers in your book.

Collecting pictures
Stick magazine pictures or postcards of wild flowers into your book. This way you can add to your record book even in the winter.

Pressing and mounting

Press only a common flower. Place it between two sheets of blotting paper and rest some heavy books on top for about a week.

When it is completely dry, put a dab of glue on the stem. Then fix it carefully to the inside of a clear plastic bag, so you can see both sides.

Stick the bag to a page in your record book with sticky tape. If you know the name of the flower, write it on the page. Write the date and place you found it as well.

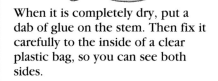

Common Fleabane

Found in a
damp meadow
on August 8th
at 11a.m.
40 cm high
21°C

A simple experiment

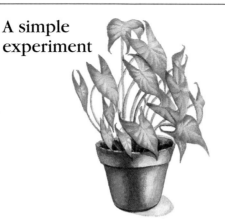

Turn a plant away from the light. In a few days time, you will see that the plant is leaning towards the

light. Plants grow towards light because they need it to make food. Plants die without light.

Make a collection of flower seeds and pods. Fix them in your book with sticky tape. Remember to label them with their flower's name.

Drawing and painting

Make coloured drawings or paintings of the quick sketches you did in your notebook when you were outside. Be sure to write down the time of day when you saw the flowers, as plants may look different in the afternoon from in the morning.

Write in your record book any information you can find about customs and festivals where flowers are used.

When flowers such as poppies or daises are in bloom, make a list of the insects that visit them. Record this in your notebook.

Leaf rubbing

Put a leaf onto a flat surface with its underside facing you.

Cover it with a piece of thin white paper. Rub backwards and forwards gently over the paper with a crayon or pencil until the shape shows through.

Stick your leaf rubbings into your record book.

Flower calendar

You will find that different plants flower at different times of the year. Make a calendar to help you remember when their flowers appear.

You will also discover that plants change appearance as the seasons change. Draw plants at different stages of their life, first when they are in bud, when the flowers come out and later when the fruits develop.

The pictures of the Arum on the right show how a plant can change its appearance, both inside and out at different stages in its life.

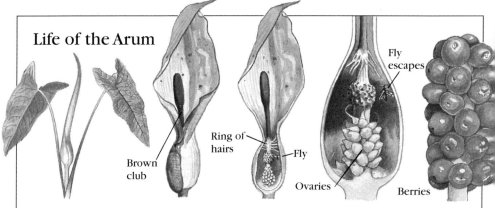

Life of the Arum

Fly escapes

Ring of hairs

Brown club

Fly

Ovaries

Berries

At first, the Arum is green. When the flower opens, it has a brown club. This attracts flies with its smell, and they get trapped inside the lower part of the flower by a ring of hairs.

The flies drop pollen on the ovaries. Then the hairs wither and the flies escape. In autumn, the ovaries become very poisonous red berries which must never be picked.

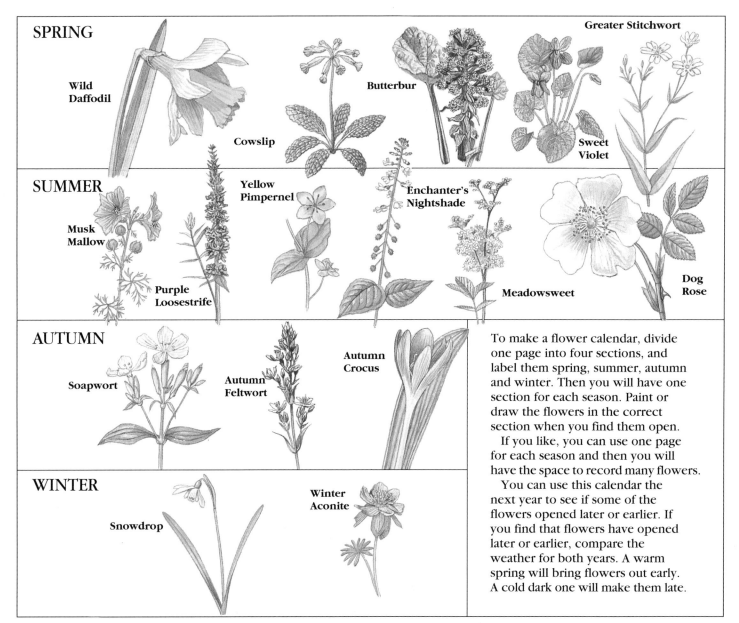

SPRING

Greater Stitchwort

Wild Daffodil

Cowslip

Butterbur

Sweet Violet

SUMMER

Yellow Pimpernel

Enchanter's Nightshade

Musk Mallow

Purple Loosestrife

Meadowsweet

Dog Rose

AUTUMN

Autumn Crocus

Soapwort

Autumn Feltwort

WINTER

Winter Aconite

Snowdrop

To make a flower calendar, divide one page into four sections, and label them spring, summer, autumn and winter. Then you will have one section for each season. Paint or draw the flowers in the correct section when you find them open.

If you like, you can use one page for each season and then you will have the space to record many flowers.

You can use this calendar the next year to see if some of the flowers opened later or earlier. If you find that flowers have opened later or earlier, compare the weather for both years. A warm spring will bring flowers out early. A cold dark one will make them late.

Rivers and ponds

Look for plants in different places around fresh water. If they actually grow in the water, they may be rooted to the bottom or their roots may float freely. Their leaves may be under the water or floating on top of it. If plants are growing on land, they may be at the water's edge, on the banks, or in swamps. Most water plants have their flowers above the water. They are usually pollinated by insects or wind, not by water.

Yellow Iris

The Yellow Iris has unusual petals and the leaves are very stiff and pointed. Look for stripes on the petals - they are nectar guides.

Frogbit

The Frogbit has shoots that grow sideways. New plants grow upwards from these shoots.

Duckweed

Duckweed can grow to cover a whole pond. It floats on top of still water.

Reedmace

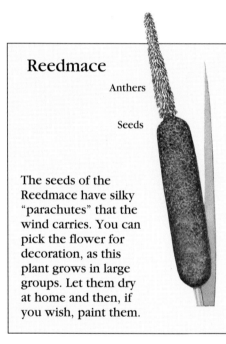

Anthers

Seeds

The seeds of the Reedmace have silky "parachutes" that the wind carries. You can pick the flower for decoration, as this plant grows in large groups. Let them dry at home and then, if you wish, paint them.

Water Lily

The petals of the Water Lily give shade to pond creatures in hot weather. They can rest on the broad, thick leaves.

Policeman's Helmet

This flower has its seeds in a fruit. When the seeds are fully grown, the fruit explodes if anything touches it. You can collect these seeds in the late summer and plant them in spring.

The leaves of fresh-water plants

The leaves of plants growing in fresh water can be all shapes and sizes - oval, round, short or long. This is because some grow under the water's surface and some on top of it, and the water itself can be still or fast-moving.

The Water Crowfoot has broad leaves above the water and thread-like leaves below the water. The Water Soldier floats completely below the water's surface.

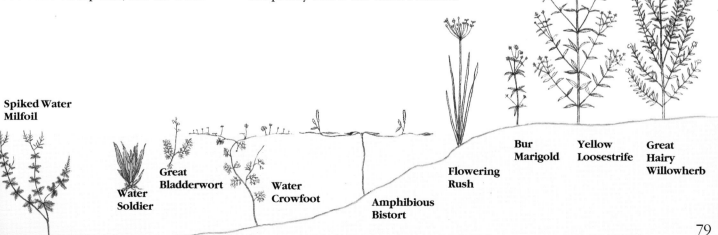

Spiked Water Milfoil

Water Soldier

Great Bladderwort

Water Crowfoot

Amphibious Bistort

Flowering Rush

Bur Marigold

Yellow Loosestrife

Great Hairy Willowherb

Fields, meadows and marshes

Some fields are used for animals to graze in and others for growing crops such as wheat and barley. You will see different flowers in different kinds of fields.

Grass grows in meadows and this is often cut to make hay. Marshes are grassy areas that are waterlogged all or almost all of the time. The flowers you find in a meadow will often be different from those you find in a marsh.

Wet soil is rich in many things that plants need to grow. This means you will find a lot of flowers in wet areas.

Marsh Marigold

This flower grows in wet meadows and looks like a large, thick-petalled buttercup.

Meadow Clary

This flower is quite common. It can be confused with Wild Clary, which has more jagged leaves and is more rare.

Marsh Thistle
The flowers are in clusters. There are prickly leaves on the dark green stems.

Yellow Rattle
When the wind blows the ripe seeds rattle inside their fruits.

Common Comfrey
The flowers are bell-shaped and hang down. You can make tea from the leaves.

Red Clover
The flower heads are made up of dozens of sweet-smelling flowers.

Wild Pansy
The flowers are violet or yellow, or a mixture of both colours.

Marsh Orchid
This plant has very unusual pink flowers. You should never pick it, or dig up the roots, as it is quite rare.

It is important to notice where flowers are growing when you find them. Marsh Orchids, for example, will often be found in the shade of a tree. Write in your notebook as many facts as possible, such as how wet or dry the soil was, if a stream was nearby, or if the land was being used for a crop or grazing animals. Often the position of a flower can be a great help when trying to identify it.

Creeping Buttercup
This plant has creeping stems which root easily.

Meadowsweet
The flowers are in clusters and smell sweet to attract insects.

Fruit

Water Avens
The sepals and petals are both red, and the flowers hang in a nodding position. The fruits are easy to spot.

Creeping Jenny
The flowers are bell-shaped and the creeping stems are matted on the ground.

Common Valerian
These red-pink flowers are common near water. They smell very unpleasant. The stem is quite stout.

Water Forget-me-Not
This plant grows near water. It is covered in soft hairs and the flower has a yellow centre.

Hedgerows and roadsides

A hedgerow is a line of specially planted bushes, usually along the edges of fields. Often other bushes start to grow in between the planted ones to give a mixture of plants. Hedgerows are important because many flowers, such as Cow Parsley, grow alongside them. As fields are cultivated and meadows mown for hay, hedgerows are often the only place left where flowers can live and grow. This means that when hedgerows are destroyed, the flowers near them usually die.

Hedgerows give shade and shelter to flowers. Often seeds are blown into a hedge and get trapped. Later they fall to the ground and start to grow.

Flowers growing on grassy verges at the roadside must be tough and strong to survive car exhaust fumes and the litter dumped on them.

Wild Clematis
The fruits have long white hairs.

Dog Rose
Birds eat the red fruits, called rosehips.

Cow Parsley
The flowers make a landing platform for insects.

Honeysuckle
The flowers are pollinated at night by moths.

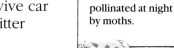

Stinging Nettle
There are stinging hairs on the leaves. The flowers are green.

Greater Burdock
The fruits stick to the fur of animals.

Dandelion
The seeds form a feathery "clock", and float away when you blow them.

Common Teasel
In winter, Common Teasels are brown and brittle.

Foxglove
These flowers are very poisonous. Do not touch them.

Fruit

Seeds

Herb Robert

Look for the fruit of the Herb Robert. When the seeds are fully grown, the fruit explodes, and the seeds shoot out.

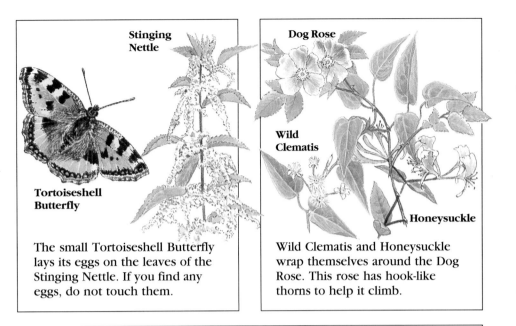

Stinging Nettle

Tortoiseshell Butterfly

The small Tortoiseshell Butterfly lays its eggs on the leaves of the Stinging Nettle. If you find any eggs, do not touch them.

Dog Rose

Wild Clematis

Honeysuckle

Wild Clematis and Honeysuckle wrap themselves around the Dog Rose. This rose has hook-like thorns to help it climb.

Make a scent jar

Make a scent jar from any flower petals that have a nice smell, such as Honeysuckle or Wild Strawberry. Put the petals between two sheets of blotting paper (picture 1) and press them under a pile of books for about a week, or until they are dry. Put the dried petals in a jar with some pieces of dried orange or lemon peel, and a bay leaf. Prepare the lid of your scent jar by punching holes with a pencil in a circle of tin foil (picture 2). Fix the foil lid carefully over and fasten it with

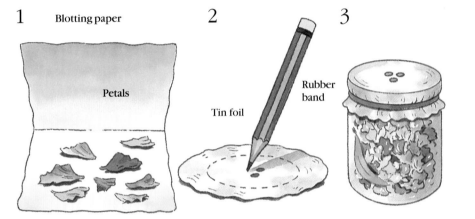

1   Blotting paper

Petals

2   Tin foil   Rubber band

3   Rubber band

a rubber band (picture 3).
   You can also put the petals in little bags that you have sewn out of fabric.

Leave one side of the bag open until you have put the dried petals inside. Then sew it up completely.

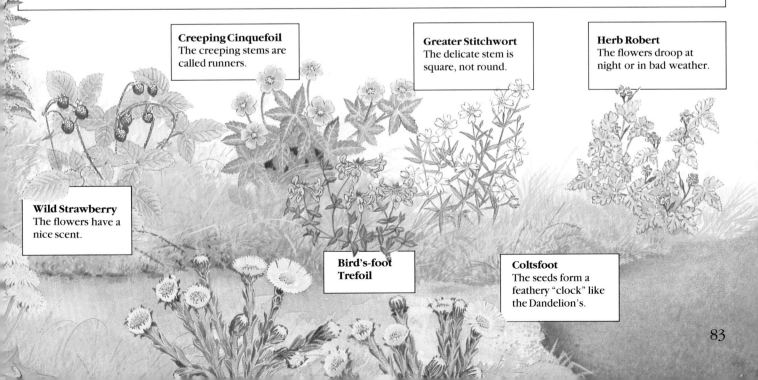

Creeping Cinquefoil
The creeping stems are called runners.

Greater Stitchwort
The delicate stem is square, not round.

Herb Robert
The flowers droop at night or in bad weather.

Wild Strawberry
The flowers have a nice scent.

Bird's-foot Trefoil

Coltsfoot
The seeds form a feathery "clock" like the Dandelion's.

Woodlands

In the summer and autumn, when all the trees are in full leaf, you will probably find only a few flowers on the ground beneath them. This is because the leaves are blocking the sunlight from reaching the flowers. The time when you usually find a lot of flowers in woodlands is in spring before the leaves have come out on the trees. Another reason for not seeing many flowers in woods is that the roots of trees take almost all the food from the soil. The kinds of flowers you will find change with the type of trees growing and the season.

At the edge of woods there will be more flowers because there is more sunlight. See for yourself how many grow near the edge and how many where it is very shady.

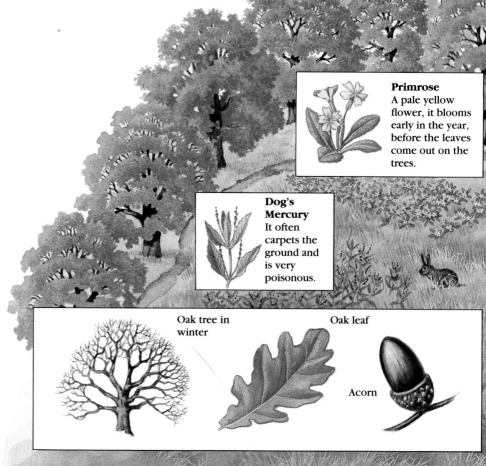

Primrose
A pale yellow flower, it blooms early in the year, before the leaves come out on the trees.

Dog's Mercury
It often carpets the ground and is very poisonous.

Oak tree in winter   Oak leaf

Acorn

Oak woods

The top picture shows an oak wood. When oak trees grow big, very little light filters down through their leaves. Even grasses find it hard to grow. A good place to hunt for flowers in an oak wood is near a path at the edge of the wood.

Beech woods

The bottom picture shows a beech wood. Beech trees grow best where the soil does not hold much water. The flowers in beech woods also prefer soil that is not too wet. See if the flowers you find in a beech wood are different from those in an oak wood.

Note

In these pictures we have left out some of the trees so you can see the flowers. In real woodlands the trees would be closer together. The scenes here are like those on the edge of woodland. Many flowers here appear before the leaves are fully out on the trees.

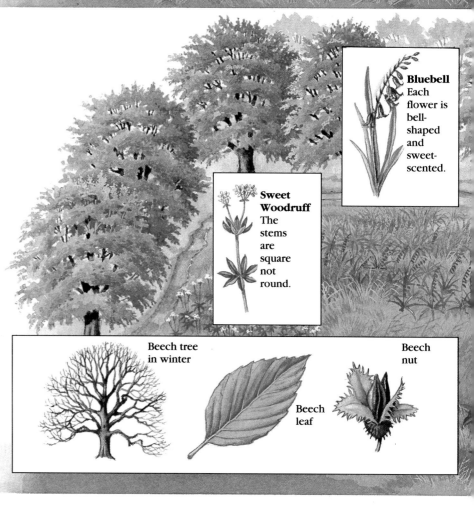

Bluebell
Each flower is bell-shaped and sweet-scented.

Sweet Woodruff
The stems are square not round.

Beech tree in winter   Beech nut

Beech leaf

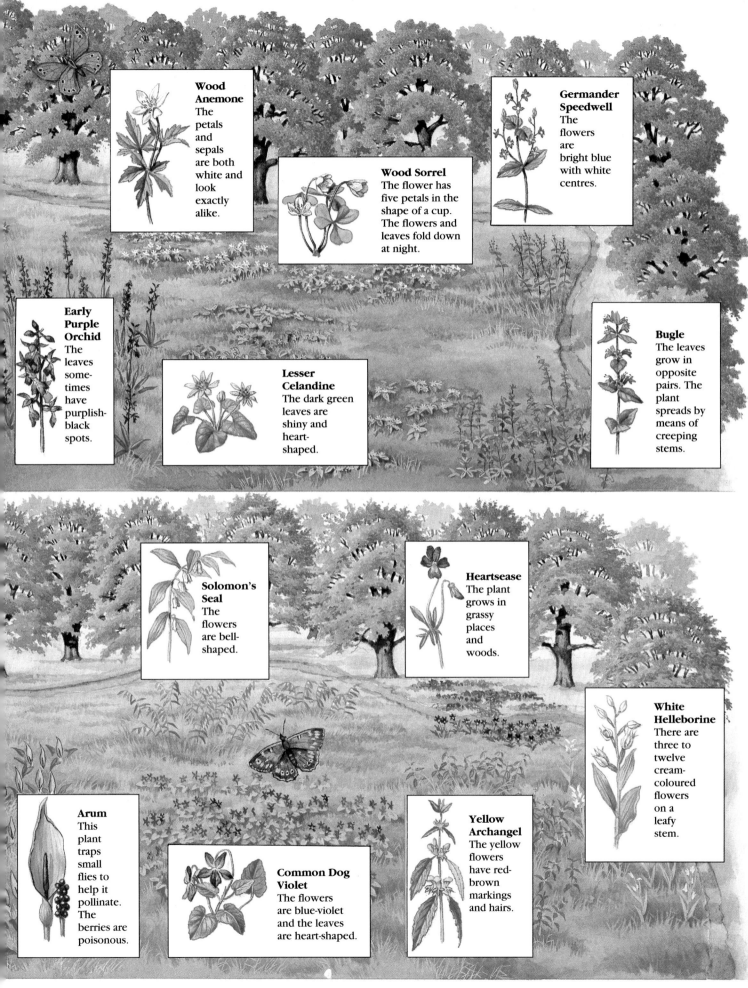

Wood Anemone The petals and sepals are both white and look exactly alike.

Wood Sorrel The flower has five petals in the shape of a cup. The flowers and leaves fold down at night.

Germander Speedwell The flowers are bright blue with white centres.

Early Purple Orchid The leaves sometimes have purplish-black spots.

Lesser Celandine The dark green leaves are shiny and heart-shaped.

Bugle The leaves grow in opposite pairs. The plant spreads by means of creeping stems.

Solomon's Seal The flowers are bell-shaped.

Heartsease The plant grows in grassy places and woods.

White Helleborine There are three to twelve cream-coloured flowers on a leafy stem.

Arum This plant traps small flies to help it pollinate. The berries are poisonous.

Common Dog Violet The flowers are blue-violet and the leaves are heart-shaped.

Yellow Archangel The yellow flowers have red-brown markings and hairs.

The seashore

Plants near the seashore must survive in very difficult conditions. The hot sun can dry them out very quickly. Strong winds can dry them out too or blow them over.

They must find ways of not losing the water inside them. To stop water escaping, some plants have a thick outer layer to trap the water, while others have a waxy coat over their leaves, or roll up their leaves when it is very hot and sunny.

Other plants may have small leaves, hairs on their leaves which shield them from the sun, or grow spines instead of leaves.

Plants must be sturdy enough not to blow over in the strong sea winds. This means they either have strong deep roots clinging onto mud, stones and rocks, or grow close to the ground so that there is less chance of them blowing over.

Salt marshes

Salt marshes are made of sand and mud. Be careful when you walk there. It is very easy to sink in. Go with a friend and wear rubber boots. The land in such places has slowly taken over from the sea. That is why the soil is salty.

There are different sections in salt marshes, called zones. Different plants grow in different zones. Many plants that grow in salt marshes do not grow further inland.

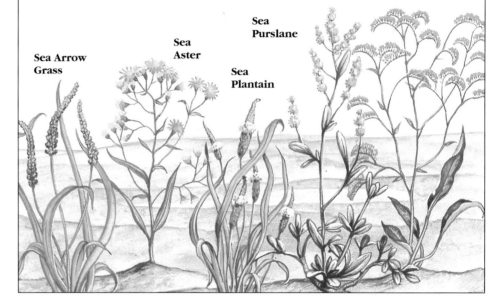

Sand dunes

Like salt marshes, sand dunes have different zones. The types of plants in each zone change according to how near the zone is to the sea and how much the dunes have been held together by plants such as Marram Grass. Couch Grass will be in a zone nearer to the sea than Ragwort.

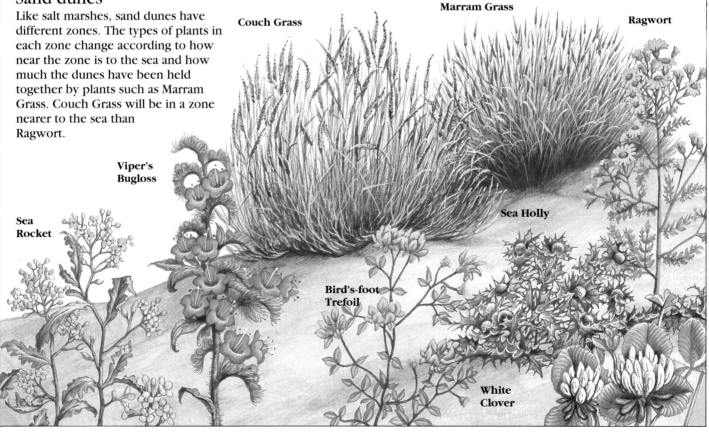

Shingle Beaches

Not many plants can grow here. These beaches are made of pebbles that once were part of cliffs or rocks. The pebbles have been worn down by the pounding of the sea. There is some sand mixed in with the pebbles, and in many places the shingle is constantly on the move. Only plants with deep roots, such as the Yellow Horned Poppy and the Sea Pea, can anchor themselves firmly enough to survive in the shingle.

Shrubby Seablite

Yellow Horned Poppy

Sea pea

Sea Bindweed

Cliffs

Plants struggle to grow here. The winds can be very fierce and blow a lot of the time. Small plants whose roots are not deep can be torn up. The rainwater drains away very quickly, leaving little for the plants. There is almost no soil. Plants must send their roots deep into cracks in the rock. Sometimes they grow along the steep sides of a cliff and can be sprayed with salty water from the sea.

Cliffs may have more soil at the top and there you may be able to find some land plants. Be careful when you look at flowers there. Do not climb any cliffs, and keep well back from the edge.

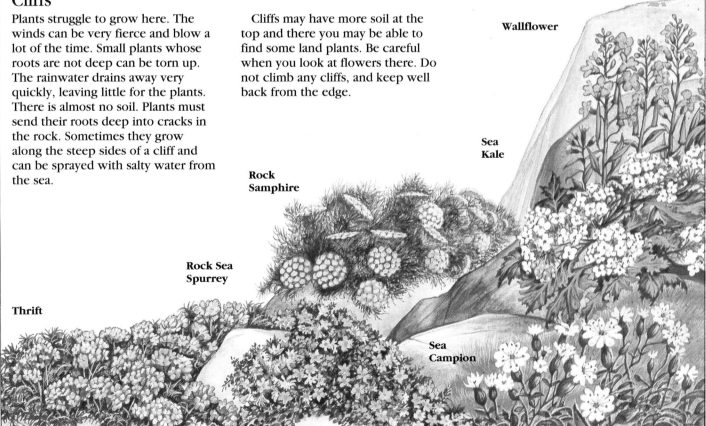

Wallflower

Sea Kale

Rock Samphire

Rock Sea Spurrey

Thrift

Sea Campion

Cities and towns

Flowers grow in waste lands, streets, car parks, gardens, on walls, or any other place in towns and cities where they can find enough soil.

Many flowers can spread quickly over open ground. Some of these flowers are called weeds. Weeds are often stronger than the plants people grow in their gardens, and they can take over. This is a big problem for gardeners.

The flowers in this section are not drawn to scale.

Seed experiment

Heat some soil in an old pan in the oven for about an hour. This will kill any seeds in the soil. Put the

pan outside. After a while do wild flowers start to grow? If so, how do you think they get there?

Wallflower
This is a garden flower, but it often "escapes" and can survive from year to year in the wild.

Pellitory of the Wall
This plant looks rather like a Stinging Nettle, but it has no stinging hairs. The stem is reddish-brown.

Ivy-leaved Toadflax
The plant is delicate and trailing, with tiny purple flowers, which have curved spurs. The stems are weak.

Prickly Sow Thistle
The leaves are spiny and clasp the stem. The flowers are pale yellow, about 2.5 cm across.

Dandelion
There is one flower head, made up of many tiny flowers, on each hollow stalk, which contains a milky juice.

Shepherd's Purse
A common weed in cities and towns. The seeds are held in a heart-shaped fruit. Flowers are white.

Ribwort Plantain
The flowers grow on small dark brown spikes. The anthers are pale yellow or purple.

White Clover
The leaves have three (and very rarely four) leaflets. The white flowers have a sweet smell to attract insects.

Common Toadflax
Each flower has an orange spot on the lower lip and a spur (a horn-shaped tube growing from a petal).

Golden Rod
The bright yellow flower heads are made up of dozens of tiny flowers. The seeds have hair parachutes.

Evening Primrose
This flower came originally from America and now grows wild in all parts of Europe.

Wall Pennywort
Look for the circular leaves on stalks - they are like tiny umbrellas. The flowers are tube-shaped.

Oxford Ragwort
The leaves have "teeth" and the flower heads grow in groups. The plant grows on bare or waste ground.

White Campion
This flower is pollinated by moths at night, and the plant has sticky hairs on it.

Rosebay Willowherb
The flowers have four bright pink petals, and the seeds have silky white hairs. They bloom from June to September.

Daisy
One of the commonest European flowers. It also grows in short grass in fields. The flowers close up at night.

Wild Chamomile
The plant spreads over wide areas, and has a nice smell when crushed. The petals may point down.

Moors and mountains

Moors

Moors are open lands that are swept by wind. Heathland is very similar. Some of these areas are very dry and some are waterlogged from time to time. Water collects in poor soil, such as in high land or near the coast. You will find fewer flowers on moors and heaths than in meadows and fields. The ones that do grow sometimes take over large sections of land.

Different flowers grow on different types of moors and heaths. The most common moorland plant is Common Heather. Sometimes it is burnt to encourage new shoots to grow. The Common Gorse is very widespread on heaths.

Alpine Bearberry
The plant has small white flowers and grows low on the ground. The unripe berries are red, and later turn blue.

Bilberry
The plant is bushy, with blue-black berries and red flowers.

Sheep's Bit
The soft blue flowers are in a rounded head and the leaves are narrow. The plant is slightly hairy.

Bog Moss
Areas covered in Bog Moss can be very wet and unsafe to walk on.

Mountains

The seeds of mountain flowers find it difficult to grow in the poor soils and the cold, windy weather of mountains. The higher up a mountain you go, the fewer flowers you will find. Trees cannot grow high up on a mountain because of the strong winds and lack of soil.

Some plants can grow high up on a mountain-side. They grow low so that the strong winds will not blow them away. Many mountain flowers spread by sending out creeping stems, which root.

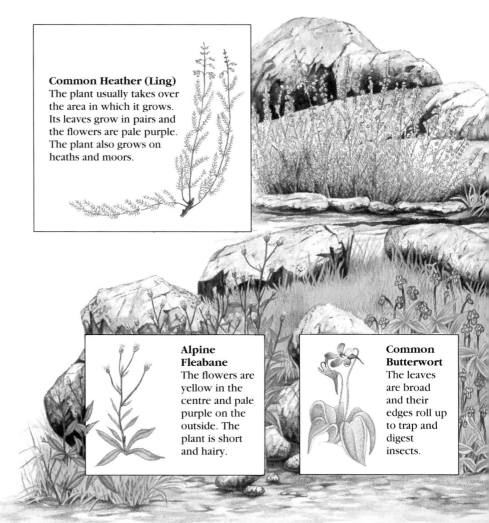

Common Heather (Ling)
The plant usually takes over the area in which it grows. Its leaves grow in pairs and the flowers are pale purple. The plant also grows on heaths and moors.

Alpine Fleabane
The flowers are yellow in the centre and pale purple on the outside. The plant is short and hairy.

Common Butterwort
The leaves are broad and their edges roll up to trap and digest insects.

Sundew
The rounded red leaves are covered with long sticky hairs that trap insects and digest them.

Bell Heather
A very common flower on heaths and moors, with needle-like leaves that grow in threes.

Starry Saxifrage
The leaves are fleshy and shiny. The tiny white flowers have pink anthers.

Harebell
The petals of the flower are joined together to form a bell shape. The flowers hang in loose bunches on long, thin stalks.

Opposite-leaved Golden Saxifrage
The leaves grow in opposite pairs on a square stem. The plant grows low on the ground.

Alpine Lady's Mantle
The leaves have silvery-grey hairs on their undersides.

Moss Campion
The leaves are tiny and pointed, and there are usually many flowers growing together, forming a thick mat on the ground.

Alpine Forget-me-Not
The plant has small blue flowers, and the leaves are soft and downy. The sepals are covered in silvery hairs.

Alpine Milk Vetch
The leaves have four to eight pairs of leaflets, and the flowers are lilac and white, often with purple tips.

Identifying flowers by colour
White flowers

Field Pennycress
30 cm. Waste ground.
Flowers in summer.

Fruit (pod)
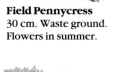

Sea Rocket
30 cm. Sandy coasts.
Flowers in summer.

Fruit

Bladder Campion
45 cm. Waste ground,
grassy places. Flowers
in spring/summer.

Greater Stitchwort
20 cm. Woods, hedges,
fields. Flowers in
spring.

Star-of-Bethlehem
15 cm. Grassy places.
Flowers in early
summer.

Cloudberry
15 cm. Upland bogs,
damp moors. Flowers
in summer.

White Stonecrop
Low and creeping. Rocks,
walls. Flowers in summer.

White Bryony
Climbs to 4 m. Hedges,
scrub. Flowers in
spring/summer.

White Dead Nettle
20 cm. Waysides,
waste places.
Flowers spring to
autumn.

Feverfew
30 cm. Walls,
waste places.
Flowers in summer.

Flower

Flower

Flower

Flower

Cow Parsley
60 cm. Hedge-banks,
shady places.
Flowers in spring.

White Melilot
60 cm. Bare and
waste ground.
Flowers in summer.

Hogweed
Up to 3 m. Grassy places,
open woods. Flowers
spring to autumn.

Daisy
10 cm. Lawns,
short grass, fields.
Flowers all year.

Yarrow
30 cm. Grassy
places. Flowers in
summer/autumn.

92 **On these pages you will find the average height of the plant from ground level to the top, the season when the plant comes into flower, and the place where it is most likely to be found.**

Yellow flowers

Bulbous Buttercup
15 cm. Grassland.
Flowers in spring.

Marsh Marigold
15 cm. Wet places.
Flowers in spring/
summer.

Yellow Horned Poppy
60 cm. Sea shingle,
waste places inland.
Flowers in summer.

Monkey Flower
20 cm. Wet
places. Flowers
in summer.

Yellow Rattle
30 cm. Grassy places,
and fields. Flowers
in spring/summer.

Wild Cabbage
60 cm. Sea cliffs.
Flowers in summer.

Silverweed
Low, creeping. Damp
grassy places. Flowers
in spring/summer.

Flower

Lady's Bedstraw
10 cm. Dry, grassy
places. Flowers
in summer.

Yellow Chamomile
30 cm. Dry, bare
and waste places.
Flowers in summer.

Groundsel
10 cm. Gardens
and waste ground.
Flowers all year.

Common Gorse
Up to 2.5 m. Heaths,
grassland.
Flowers all year.

Common Rockrose
Close to the ground.
Grassy and rocky places.
Flowers in summer.

Flower

Kidney Vetch
15 cm. Dry grassland,
by sea, mountains.
Flowers spring/summer.

**Perforate St John's
Wort**
45 cm. Grassy places.
Flowers in summer.

Yellow Water Lily
4 cm above water. Still
water, slow streams.
Flowers in summer.

**Remember - if you cannot see a picture of the flower you want to identify here, then look on the pages earlier in this section which
link flowers with the places where they grow.**

Pink and red flowers

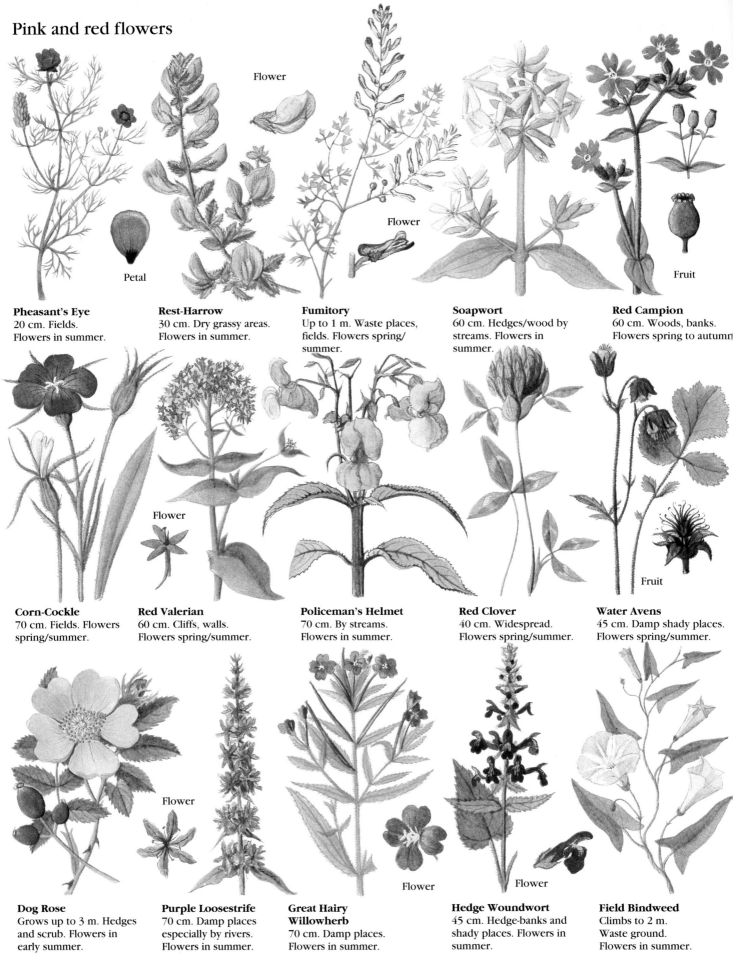

Flower

Petal

Flower

Flower

Fruit

Pheasant's Eye
20 cm. Fields.
Flowers in summer.

Rest-Harrow
30 cm. Dry grassy areas.
Flowers in summer.

Fumitory
Up to 1 m. Waste places,
fields. Flowers spring/
summer.

Soapwort
60 cm. Hedges/wood by
streams. Flowers in
summer.

Red Campion
60 cm. Woods, banks.
Flowers spring to autumn

Flower

Fruit

Corn-Cockle
70 cm. Fields. Flowers
spring/summer.

Red Valerian
60 cm. Cliffs, walls.
Flowers spring/summer.

Policeman's Helmet
70 cm. By streams.
Flowers in summer.

Red Clover
40 cm. Widespread.
Flowers spring/summer.

Water Avens
45 cm. Damp shady places.
Flowers spring/summer.

Flower

Flower

Flower

Dog Rose
Grows up to 3 m. Hedges
and scrub. Flowers in
early summer.

Purple Loosestrife
70 cm. Damp places
especially by rivers.
Flowers in summer.

**Great Hairy
Willowherb**
70 cm. Damp places.
Flowers in summer.

Hedge Woundwort
45 cm. Hedge-banks and
shady places. Flowers in
summer.

Field Bindweed
Climbs to 2 m.
Waste ground.
Flowers in summer.

On these pages you will find the average height of the plant from ground level to the top, the season when the plant comes into
flower, and the place where it is most likely to be found.

Blue and mauve flowers

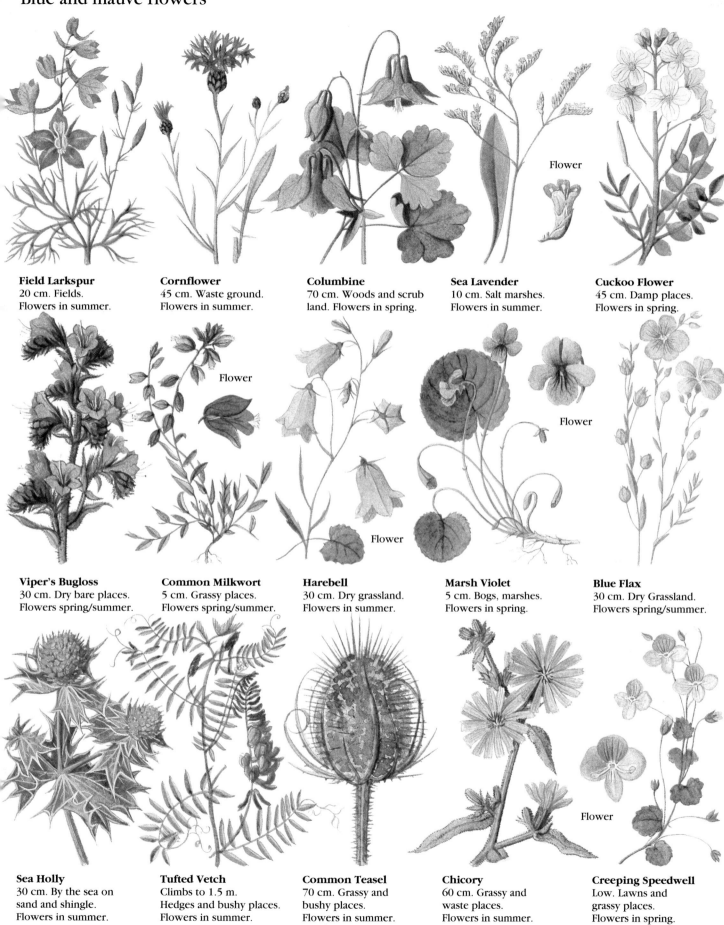

Field Larkspur
20 cm. Fields.
Flowers in summer.

Cornflower
45 cm. Waste ground.
Flowers in summer.

Columbine
70 cm. Woods and scrub
land. Flowers in spring.

Sea Lavender
10 cm. Salt marshes.
Flowers in summer.

Flower

Cuckoo Flower
45 cm. Damp places.
Flowers in spring.

Flower

Flower

Flower

Viper's Bugloss
30 cm. Dry bare places.
Flowers spring/summer.

Common Milkwort
5 cm. Grassy places.
Flowers spring/summer.

Harebell
30 cm. Dry grassland.
Flowers in summer.

Marsh Violet
5 cm. Bogs, marshes.
Flowers in spring.

Blue Flax
30 cm. Dry Grassland.
Flowers spring/summer.

Flower

Sea Holly
30 cm. By the sea on
sand and shingle.
Flowers in summer.

Tufted Vetch
Climbs to 1.5 m.
Hedges and bushy places.
Flowers in summer.

Common Teasel
70 cm. Grassy and
bushy places.
Flowers in summer.

Chicory
60 cm. Grassy and
waste places.
Flowers in summer.

Creeping Speedwell
Low. Lawns and
grassy places.
Flowers in spring.

Remember - if you cannot see a picture of the flower you want to identify here, then look on the pages earlier in this section which link flowers with the places where they grow.

Index